Secre
Forever
Happiness

Books by Roy Eugene Davis

An Easy Guide to Meditation
How You Can Use the Technique of Creative
 Imagination
This Is Reality
The Science of Kriya Yoga
The Philosophy & Practice of Yoga
The Christ of God: Light of the World
How to Pray: With Results Following
God Has Given Us Every Good Thing
Our Awakening World
Open Your Life to Infinite Good
Studies in Truth
Secrets of Inner Power
Time, Space & Circumstance
Miracle Man of Japan

Secrets of Forever Happiness

A Holistic Guide to Permanent Fulfillment Through Spiritual Growth and Responsible Living

by Roy Eugene Davis

FELL PUBLISHERS, INC.
Hollywood, Florida

Library of Congress Cataloging-in-Publication Data

Davis, Roy Eugene.
    The secrets of forever happiness / by Roy Eugene Davis.
      p.   cm.
    ISBN 0-8119-0032-0 (pbk.): $7.95
    1. Spiritual life.   2. Happiness   I. Title.
    BL624.D319 1990
    291.4'48—dc20   88-83602
                                                                      CIP

International Standard Book Number: 0-8119-0032-0
Library of Congress Catalog Card Number: 88-83602

For information address:

Fell Publishers, Inc.
2131 Hollywood Boulevard
Hollywood, Florida 33020

Published simultaneously in Canada by Prentice-Hall
Canada, Toronto, Canada

Manufactured in the United States of America
1 2 3 4 5 6 7 8 9 0

CONTENTS

INTRODUCTION

True happiness is the theme of this book; not memorable good times, not possible future satisfaction, but happiness based on inner understanding and soul peace.

In the following pages I have explained procedures for living which are acceptable to everyone, regardless of present circumstances, and which can contribute to self-understanding, a harmonious relationship with the world, and the fulfillment of life's purposes. These principles, being natural and universal, apply equally to all of us—to you, to me, to the people we know.

Right understanding of our relationship with God is emphasized because it is the basic essential to forever happiness. Right ways of living are explained because they are necessary to our being at peace with our world and to remaining in a healthy condition. Other things not covered in this book will certainly be discovered by the reader as he or she unfolds inborn capacities to experience ever-increasing levels of awareness and insight. When we are in tune with life, the universe itself proves to be our friend, our protector and provider, and the vehicle of grace.

Some of the material found in Chapter Six is taken from one of my earlier books *(Our Awakening World: Handbook of Spiritual Practices & Guide to Radiant Living in the New Era,* published by CSA Press, Lakemont, Georgia) and is included here because I consider it important to the theme. While it is true that happiness is experienced inwardly, at the level of being, it is also necessary for us to actualize our hopes and dreams in this world. For this reason, strategies which can contribute to wellness on all levels are included in Chapter Six, and supporting routines are included in the chapters preceding it.

The mere publishing and wide distribution of this book will not solve the problems of all who read it. Only the reader can decide upon a reasonable course of action and, by so doing, put into practice what is here suggested in order to experience benefits.

What you will learn here is what you already know at a deeper level of your being, because knowledge of life is grounded in our own consciousness. What we need is to contemplate deeply, bring forth dormant knowledge, and apply it with reason. Only when we enter into the process of living do we have the opportunity to fully discover our place in the universe and, by so doing, fulfill our personal destinies.

I was fortunate, during my teenage years, to have the courage to begin an exhaustive search for the meaning of life—through prayer and reflection, in books, and by meeting role models who shared their understanding with me and provided encouragement. In my eighteenth year I met my guru, Paramahansa Yogananda, in Los Angeles, California. After a few years of study and practice I was led to teach, not my own wisdom, but the basic truths of life long taught by seers of the ages.

I hope that all who read this book will take to heart the message, then follow through with total commitment to experience inner growth and forever happiness.

ROY EUGENE DAVIS

March, 1990
Lakemont, Georgia

Note: To contact the author, write: c/o Center for Spiritual Awareness, Box 7, Lake Rabun Road, Lakemont, Georgia 30552 (U.S.A.)

Happy is the man that findeth wisdom, and the man that getteth understanding.

-*Proverbs 3:13*

If happiness is activity in accordance with excellence, it is reasonable that it should be in accordance with the highest excellence.

-*Aristotle*

O happiness! our being's end and aim!
Good, pleasure, ease, content! whate'er thy name:
That something still which prompts the eternal sigh,
For which we bear to live or dare to die.

-*Alexander Pope*

That action is best which procures the greatest happiness for the greatest numbers.

-*Francis Hutcheson*

CHAPTER 1

The Only Basis for True and Lasting Happiness

I offer you the supreme treasure, the way to true and lasting happiness. This is my gift to you. It is given freely. I expect nothing in return, because I know your happiness will be your eternal blessing, and because of it, others will become happy.

Happiness cannot be bargained for—it can only be accepted. It can be the easiest thing of all to accept, yet for many it is the most difficult. Easy, because it *already* exists within us at the level of being. Difficult, because personal attitudes and conditioned behavior often prevent us from acknowledging and experiencing it.

Whenever I write about these matters, as I often do, and whenever I speak about them to groups, which is frequent, I always prepare myself by being quiet for a few minutes and opening myself to inner guidance. At

such times these words float in my mind: "Keep it simple, keep it God-centered." What follows, therefore,
will be simple and it will be God-centered.

Do not let the word *God* dissuade you. It is but a
word we use to refer to the Higher Power, the One life,
the Cosmic Essence, the Larger Self of each of us and of
all that is. Without an understanding of this Beingness,
no real happiness is possible.

I am making this clear from the beginning so that
you will know ahead of time what must be understood.
As we proceed you will learn what can be done to understand more about It, more about what your inner
nature really is, and how you can experience a conscious and permanent relationship with God.

This is not a book about religion. Here you will
find no sectarian bias; here are no "shoulds" and
"should nots," except as these relate to assisting you to
live more in harmony with natural laws in order to fulfill your worthy purposes and grow in the direction of
emotional and spiritual maturity. What is offered in
these pages will be acceptable to every reader who sincerely desires to experience fulfillment, regardless of
his or her cultural origins, life style or circumstances,
and whether he or she is presently "religious" or not.

While we differ in attitudes, beliefs, and circumstances for a variety of reasons, at a deeper level we are
all the same. We have similar physiological or physical-
chemistry characteristics, with brains, nervous systems, organs, glands and internal systems much alike.
We all have mental capacities and emotional drives. We
even have common urges and desires: we want to be secure, functional, healthy and successful, fulfilling our
reasonable expectations and accomplishing our useful

purposes. Furthermore, sooner or later we will want to know, and will not be satisfied until we do know, our place in the universe and our relationship to God. We will consider these matters in the following pages, emphasizing those matters which are relevant to higher purposes, and avoiding those which are not. Think of this book as your handbook, a working manual to be studied and used to assist you in unfolding your inborn capacities.

Within you, and within every person, are virtually limitless capacities to be awakened and actualized. This is so because, at the deep level of being, we are grounded in an unbounded field of pure existence, out of which nature emerges and by which nature is sustained and nourished. Your understanding of this fact will increase as you enter into a process of growth as the result of personal application of the principles and procedures here offered.

You will be reminded of what you already inwardly know at the deep inner level of your being, because knowledge already resides here. This knowledge and how to correctly utilize it, will emerge into your conscious awareness as you proceed. This is how learning occurs. It unfolds from within us as we study, learn, and put what we learn into practice. To encourage the emergence of knowledge you must take to heart what is here shared and make it your own through personal practice.

Only a Holistic Approach to Living Through Learning Will Fully Satisfy

The time-tested way here offered is not for the person who is thinking in terms of quickly being the person he wants to be, doing the whimsical things he wants to do, or having egocentric dominance over his environment. The way offered is for the person who is sincerely willing to come to terms with the forces of the universe and learn to consciously cooperate with them. In this way personal fulfillment and fulfillment of soul destiny are assured.

Because of the importance of complete fulfillment based on inner happiness and appropriate behavior, all levels of experience and function will be addressed. First among these is the matter of correct understanding of who and what we really are, as units of consciousness, and the means to encourage spiritual growth and awareness, without which no outer attainment will be complete.

Everything I share in this book I once learned and then applied; nothing recommended here is second-hand knowledge. I have done, and do, the things I write about, and I am still in the process of doing and learning. Do not err in falsely assuming that this information and these instructions cannot possibly apply to you. If you are not yet grounded in true happiness, experiencing life from the center of your being, everything you read in the following pages will be useful to you. Pass nothing by; read this book again and again, be certain of the definitions of special words, be diligent in the use of the self-evaluation sections and review sections, and practice every technique and use every procedure. Let your own personal experience confirm the usefulness of what you learn. In this way you will actualize—make real in your life—what you learn, and you will experience a partnership with the creative force of the universe.

Be humble as you proceed, willing to release non-useful ways of thinking and behaving. Accept the fact that sometimes growth will be pleasurable and sometimes it will be, in varying degrees, painful. Growth can be pleasurable when insight and increased freedom of function occur, but it can be painful when conflict is present. If pleasure occurs, let it be—but do not cling to it. If pain is experienced, know that you will move through it—this, too, will pass away. Perceptions and circumstances change with the ebb and flow of nature.

The boundaries of your ego will slowly, or perhaps quickly, dissolve as you continue on your awakening way. You will inevitably become more expansive, more mentally clear, more aware, more cosmicly conscious. This cannot be avoided as we mature. The gift of grace is a great blessing, the natural result of the emergence of inner qualities and capacities. You will, more and more, look upon living as an adventure, and you will become increasingly conscious of your foreverness.

Many people, millions of them in fact, (and I say this without judgment of any kind) are totally involved with petty personal concerns. They are struggling to survive, coping with circumstances, driven by urges and tendencies rooted deep in their unconscious. Millions, too, are reasonably sane, reasonably functional, and yet compulsively involved in "proving" themselves from the basis of ego identification. Does what is offered in this book offer any hope to them? Yes, because no matter from where we begin, if we are sincere and intent, progress will occur. No matter what your present circumstances may be, here are the keys to self-understanding and growth possibilities. The highly educated and the uneducated, the success and the failure, the free and the presently restricted, the well and the sick—all have equal opportunity to learn and to take a hand in their own inner transformation and enlightenment. This *way* is not for a few; it is ultimately for every person, and while one may enjoy the support of friends on the path, the way is that of aloneness. But it is an aloneness in which one need never be lonely.

The Happiness We Seek Is Already Within Us

Let us clearly understand this basic premise, basic because it is true—*lasting happiness can never be experienced in relationship to externals*. Our relationships with others, as satisfying as they may be at times, are always subject to change, because time is an ingredient of nature. This is not to say that harmonious and supportive relationships should not be cultivated and enjoyed, or that we should withdraw from participation in normal affairs, but we should remember that the kind of happiness which is constant is innate to us at the level of being. All other sensations we may describe as happiness—contentment, serenity, satisfaction, gladness, joy—are impermanent when associated with external relationships, circumstances or emotions.

It becomes obvious to us when we exercise our faculty of reason that we are in this world to learn, to grow, and to function as mature beings in a universe which itself is undergoing transformation in the direction of completing the purpose for it. All life forms grow, mature and eventually pass from the visible to the invisible. In the course of time we, too, as physical expressions, will pass from the mortal scene. The beingness of us, however, will continue to unfold and express. So far as we know, man alone, among all the creatures of Earth, has the capacity to extend awareness beyond physical and psychological limits to know conscious spiritual freedom as the inevitable result of comprehending his true essence and its relationship to the whole.

In writing this book I have taken the long-range view that we are preparing ourselves for future possibilities, but the principles and procedures I share will work just as well for that reader who is presently thinking in terms of short-term benefits, or of making it through to reasonably advanced years in a healthy condition of spirit, mind and body.

There is no need to strain as we proceed. We can take purely on faith that which seems useful, then acquire experience by doing. Our inner intelligence will lead us correctly as we do our part to help ourselves in the direction of fulfillment.

There is also the matter of *grace*. While grace may at times seem to originate outside of us, really it does not. The source of grace is the field of Pure Being, which is also our source. But grace does operate outside of our minds and personalities, in that it manifests through us and around us because of the creative force which is responsible for the maintenance of all aspects of the universe, and for all life-expressions in the universe, including you and me.

Grace occurs when we expect it, if we are sufficiently open and responsive to it; it occurs when we do not expect it, and when we may not even be aware of its existence or operation. It is that "something" which causes beneficial things to occur without our causing them. It can contribute to an adjustment of difficult circumstances, to unusual healings, to sudden insights and spiritual awakening, and to the averting of accidents and the provision of helpful friends or needed resources just when we need these most. Indeed, as we become more responsive to it, grace never fails, because the impulse of life to fulfill its purposes cannot fail.

This is why it is extremely wise to make sure that our known purposes are in harmony with life's purposes. If our purposes are in harmony with life's purposes, grace will contribute to their unfoldment. If they are not, grace will intervene to set us on the right course, sooner or later.

We will speak of worthy purpose later, and how to know and flow with it. For now we will only mention that clear direction in life follows purpose. It is therefore wise for us to train ourselves to be disciplined and to avoid those involvements which can in no way contribute to our growth. Various theories, notions, systems, and "ways" to actualize inborn capacities frequently emerge on the public scene and are promoted as rapid ways to fulfillment. They quickly pass and are forgotten because they neither meet needs nor hold up under careful scrutiny.

While it can be enjoyable to study and examine many possibilities, and temporarily satisfying to travel and to seek out the meaning of life, what we seek to know has been known for ages, and what is to be experienced is present where we are. Regardless of the outer drama currently unfolding, the beingness of us ever remains what it is. It is this we must acknowledge and experience, and the degree to which we do it will determine the degree of true happiness we will know.

The common saying, "a person can be as happy as he decides to be," is perhaps so often quoted because it happens to be true. Unless you undergo an instant illumination experience, you will seldom actually experience your beingness merely by deciding to do so; but you can begin the process by deciding to cultivate inner peace and contentment regardless of past personal history or present circumstances. You can then be resolved to learn how to know true happiness and enter into the process which can assure it.

What 500 People Said When Asked About Happiness

Before starting the actual writing of this book, I sent a form letter to 1200 men and women in North America asking them to answer a list of questions on the subject of happiness. Within three weeks I received some 500 responses. The careful attention given to answering the questions indicated much personal interest in the project, and I am grateful to each person who responded.

Although persons polled were residents of the U.S. and Canada, with a few in Mexico and the Caribbean islands, they represent the aspirations and moods of the planet's population in general. This statement is based on the fact that in travels to Japan, South America, England, Europe and West Africa, I have found similar aspirations, emotional states, and personal needs. Because all of those contacted were on my mailing list, I knew ahead of time their interest in self-improvement and spiritual awareness. Except for this common interest, they represented a wide divergence of lifestyles and interests. Among them were homemakers, office and factory workers, computer programmers, lawyers, medical doctors, chiropractors, nurses, airline attendants and pilots, truck drivers, construction workers, ministers, dentists, high school and college teachers and students, and publishers. Some were retired but actively involved in personal interests or community service. Approximately 65% were females and 35% males. Ages ranged from 20 to 86, with the average age being 53. Therefore, the survey was fairly representative of the general population. About 65% were married and the rest were either single, divorced or had survived a spouse. Eighty-five percent reported good health, most of the rest fair health, and only a very few claimed their health was poor.

The first question asked was, *"What is your personal definition of happiness?"* Answers varied: living each moment, being inwardly satisfied, doing my best, loving God, being able to help others, being financially secure, and feeling good about myself and others were a few answers.

To the question, *"Do you consider yourself to be a happy person?"* about 70% said they did, a few said they did not, and several chose not to respond to the question.

In response to the question, *If you are not presently happy, what do you think would make you happy?"* the answers were similar to those given for the first question, although several did mention a better awareness of the presence of God as a choice.

When asked, *"What do you think are some of the major problems or challenges people face in today's world, or in general in living their lives?"* the answers ranged from that of not knowing their inner nature, to poverty, threat of war, selfishness, drugs, and crime.

Very few admitted to having any fears, and only the few who said they were unhappy seemed to have any major problems. Eighty percent claimed to be religious, although not necessarily involved with a traditional church. Of those who said they were not religious, most were in some way involved with increasing their spiritual awareness. An overwhelming number stated they were engaged in spiritual practices of one kind or another.

Twenty percent were satisfied with their level of spiritual understanding and the rest were not. About the same number were satisfied or dissatisfied with their degree of mental clarity and ability.

About 40% were as emotionally calm as they wanted to be. About the same number said they were as physically vital as desired. Most claimed good human relationships and said they were comfortable living in the world. To the question, *"Are you as prosperous as you would like to be?"* only 40% said they were prosperous, while 60% said they were not. In spite of the fact that 60% or more said they were not as spiritually aware, emotionally calm, mentally clear, or prosperous as they would like to be, *a full 80% of respondents claimed to be as successful as they would like to be!* About 75% admitted to paying attention to nutritional needs. Ninety-two percent felt it is possible to know true and lasting happiness in this world; eight percent felt otherwise.

In all, among those who responded, a willingness to prevail was strongly evident, as well as an obvious need for many to become more spiritually aware, more emotionally content, more mentally clear, and more prosperous. The response was about what I thought it might be, with only one or two exceptions, and the findings have contributed greatly to certain themes found in later chapters of this book.

The Heart's Sincere Desire, the Yearning of Every Soul

I am convinced that the sincere desire, the yearning, of every person at the level of being is to live free in an unbounded universe. Further, this is the "promise" of philosopher-seers of the ages, those who claimed to have had an inner vision of man's possibilities. It is the certain knowing of my heart, my essence, as it is the knowing and the aspiration of many with whom I have shared occasions of honest conversation.

What could be more natural than for us to desire to be all we can be and to move through space-time as easily as we dream we can? What could be more natural than to manifest innate capacities and to share with the world the best of life there is? Cannot righteousness prevail on earth, or must there forever be contention, strife, and the challenge of dire threats to orderly life?

I envision a world in which the majority of inhabitants flow with the rhythms of nature and in which mutual love rules. I am not the only dreamer of this possible dream, for increasing numbers also share it. The hope that springs from the heart, from the beingness of us, is prompted by impulses which are purely divine in origin.

What hopes and dreams do you have, for yourself and your world? What worthy purposes do you serve? What selfless goals do you have and how will you achieve them? What present problems do you perceive and how will they be solved? *What do you really want to experience during your remaining years on Planet Earth?* Think on these things, knowing that within you, and around you, is *that* which can make possible all of which you are worthy, all those things which you will prepare yourself to experience. If you want to be happy, you will be happy. If you want to be healthy, you will be healthy. If you want to be the servant of all, you will be the servant of all—which is one secret of forever happiness.

Review

1. God is the Higher Power, the One Life, the Cosmic Essence, the Larger Self of every person and every creature.
2. You will never be satisfied until you know your relationship with God and your true place in the universe.
3. As the boundaries of your ego dissolve, you will become more expansive, more mentally clear, more aware, more cosmicly conscious.
4. Lasting happiness can never be experienced in relationship to externals. Lasting happiness is experienced at the inner level of being.
5. Grace is the activity of the Holy Spirit (the life of God) moving in, through and around us to transform and regenerate.
6. The sincere desire, the yearning, of every person at the level of being is to live free in an unbounded universe.

SELF-EVALUATION AND PLANNING

1. What do you want to experience or do during your remaining years on Planet Earth?

2. What are you willing to do to allow experience and projects to unfold?

3. Write a list of your present talents and abilities.

4. What, if anything, is limiting you, and what are you willing to do to clear these restrictions from your life?

In the beginning God created the heaven and the earth—And God said, Let there be light: and there was light.

—*Genesis 1:1 & 3*

And whosoever, either now or after I am gone, shall be a lamp unto themselves, and a refuge unto themselves, shall betake themselves to no external refuge, but, holding fast to the truth as their lamp...it is they who shall reach the topmost height. But, they must be anxious to learn.

—*The Buddha*

The path of God is eternal. The soul is immortal. God permeates the soul with his divine attributes. Let the soul journey on the path of God in constant communion with him.

—*Lahiri Mahasaya*

On this road, therefore, to abandon one's own way is to enter the true way, or, to speak more correctly, to pass onwards to the goal; and to forsake one's own way is to enter on that which has none, namely, God.

—*St. John of the Cross*

CHAPTER 2

How to Definitely Experience Inner Growth and Spiritual Awareness

If you sincerely want to experience inner growth and steady unfoldment of innate capacities, study this chapter carefully, and diligently apply the recommended procedures. This information comprises the inner knowledge which forms the basis of every mature philosophical-religious-enlightenment tradition of the world. The understanding of it will satisfy the heart as well as the intellect.

We must start at the beginning to discover where we presently are, and why. We can then prepare ourselves to actually comprehend and experience what has been explained. For some of you, much of this material will already be familiar, while for others, it will be new. If you have been exposed to these ideas before, examine them again to deepen your understanding. If these ideas are new to you, exercise your powers of intelligence and listen to the response of your inner nature. In this way you may discern the inner meaning of what you read and acquire insights which will be extremely helpful in making your life more worthwhile.

Relative aspects of nature are more comprehensible if we understand, even in part, the absolute basis underlying manifestation of all relative occurrences. Nature is supported by something, and this something is the field of pure consciousness from which impulses arise to make manifestation possible.

The pure field of consciousness is *unmodified* being, which is why we refer to it as pure. Relative manifestations are "mixed"; that is, they are made possible by the interaction of cosmic forces which express from fine, to subtle, to gross levels. There is currently some debate among scientists as to whether the universe had a "big bang" to start it off, or whether it has always been. Perhaps, the alternative theory goes, the stuff of manifest form has always been present, as unformed matter, electricity and magnetism. This seems plausible and would allow for a dramatic beginning in the direction of gross manifestation, while also providing an explanation for the basis of manifestation. In fact, many ancient scriptures assert that world manifestation occurs, persists for billions of years, then recedes for a duration, only to manifest again. The beginningless existence of fine forces would allow for this process, without compromising the theory of instantaneous creation of matter. It is currently believed that over 90% of all matter is formless and pervades the universe. Manifestation, then, seems to be steadily occurring, just as gross matter is steadily decaying as its finer forces are released to return to the unmanifest field of unformed matter-substance.

Let us assume that from the field of pure consciousness impulses arise to manifest as creative force, which further interacts upon itself to express as fine, subatomic particles. From these particles atoms are formed, then molecules, then structured matter. This makes possible the stage upon which the game of life takes place.

Consider, then, that life impulses interact with fine matter to create animate forms, single-celled organisms, more complex organisms and, because of the process of growth, all of the even more complex organisms. In this way nature unfolds, and life units ensoul suitable forms and organisms.

With the understanding that from the field of pure consciousness, which is self-contained and self-enlivened, emerge both the ingredients making nature possible and the life essence capable of animating suitable forms and organisms, we can comprehend the world around us. We do not have to engage in theological speculation to examine our world in this way. We can, instead, begin to discern the marvelous simplicity of the process and, with patient study, eventually learn what our role in the overall scheme is.

Here, then, is the picture: a single reality, pure consciousness, is responsible for giving rise to a single force which, because of innate tendencies caused by polarities, acts upon itself to manifest the universe and enliven it. This answers such questions as, "How did it happen," and "Why are we here?" Knowing this does not solve the problem of how to prepare ourselves to more fully comprehend the entire range of consciousness, unmanifest and manifest. We shall learn to solve these problems as we proceed in this chapter.

The innate tendencies, or attributes, pervading all of nature and at work within us, are three in number: the tendency in the direction of the pure field of consciousness, which contributes to transformation, human aspiration, spiritual growth, and enlightenment; the tendency to action, which allows movement, transformation, and change; and the tendency to inertia, which contributes to heaviness, the binding or cohesion of cosmic forces, and dullness and lack of consciousness in human beings and all life forms. The ideal for one on the enlightenment path is to work with these tendencies, experience harmony with nature, aspire to right action and understanding, and eventually rise above their influence entirely.

The Universe is a Continuum, a Series of Related Aspects

When we examine our world objectively, from our present point of view we see an almost infinite variety of manifestations, and we often differentiate among them. When viewed subjectively, however, as the result of inner contemplation leading to insight, the universe is discerned as one thing—a series of related aspects. This is why some refer to it as a "cosmic dance," one that is forever occurring.

Often we feel we are distinct from our environment, when in fact, we are not. Cosmic forces originating in distant space flow through our minds and bodies, and our thought impulses and physical energies flow out to interact with the mental field and material energies of the universe. While we may believe we are confined to a form of flesh, we are really particularized units of pure consciousness, and our bodies are part of the cosmic body. We are constantly interacting with the outer universe. This is why it is important for us to learn to be in harmony with internal forces and with our environment. By learning to be grounded in inner happiness, the pure state of our being, we place ourselves in the most ideal state from which to act in order to experience harmony with others and with all aspects of nature.

Originating in the source—the field of pure consciousness—and pervading the entire universe, is the creative impulse to express. This is the force driving the process of evolution. Because this trend is persistent, nature possesses an innate support system which ensures ordered activity and the completion of creative trends. This is why seers have long taught that there is a "way of righteousness" uniformly pervading the universe and that man can learn to be open to it and cooperate with it. The process by which a person can learn to harmonize with the supportive influences available to him is referred to as "the eternal way of righteousness which ever was, is, and will ever be." It is not subject to personal whims or to beliefs or disbeliefs of individuals. It is always what it is. Any person who aspires to experience a relationship with it can learn to do so. All that is needed is right understanding and correct involvement.

Whether we know it or not, when we refer to God we are referring to the one life, being, intelligence and power which alone is responsible for all manifestation. When we think of God, or pray to God, regardless of our present understanding of God, we are opening ourselves to a greater measure of relationship to the one life. It cannot in any way be influenced by what we think about it or by what words we use to refer to it.

Why We May Not Consciously Know Our True Nature

The question may arise, "If we are, at the inmost center of being, specialized units of pure consciousness, why is it that we are not more aware of this?"

Here is the reason, the understanding of which will enable you to do something about your own inner growth and increase of spiritual awareness. When units of pure consciousness (souls) identify with subtle matter as the result of having been impelled outward by impulses from the field of pure consciousness, such identification becomes so nearly complete that awareness is partially diminished, causing the being to assume itself to be that with which it identifies.

Have you not often felt yourself to be a body, with a mind and, perhaps, a soul? Many religious people speak of their concern about saving their souls, as though the soul, which is their very being, was something apart from them. This error in perception is the major problem and the cause of personal unknowing or delusion. We say a person is deluded when he or she obviously does not comprehend the truth about something, especially when the person concludes that the

facts about the subject are known to him, when they are not.
Planet Earth presently has an ever increasing human population of over five billion. Among the human family are many who are almost completely unconscious, many who are partially conscious, many who are quite conscious, a great many who are rapidly awakening, and surely many who are either fully enlightened or very nearly so. To be enlightened is to be knowledgeable, to comprehend. There are, of course, degrees of enlightenment, and when I refer to the "enlightenment path" I refer to that course of action to which one is committed with the intention of awakening to total comprehension of the nature and characteristics of consciousness, from the pure field of unmanifest existence through to universal manifestation. This is the final "truth" which enables you to be free— free from unknowingness and free to live without restrictions in a supportive cosmos.

The inborn inclination of every person is to be able to fulfill all duties necessary to ensure the satisfaction of needs, to relate to the world harmoniously, and to achieve worthy purposes. Inner growth, psychological maturity and spiritual awareness enable us to do all of these.

Regardless of your present degree of spiritual awareness and personal understanding, you can begin from that place and constructively contribute to the learning and unfolding process. For this it is helpful for you to be a *disciple* on the enlightenment path. With this attitude you are open to inner guidance which will reveal circumstances in life which can be understood as growth opportunities. In fact, all present and future life circumstances can be accepted as the school in which we learn our lessons and become increasingly knowledgeable and competent.

Obviously, not everyone in this world is presently interested in entering into a process of self-transformation and enlightenment. Many are overwhelmed by circumstances and at the mercy of inner conflicts, and if they can survive by coping, they feel they have accomplished something worthwhile. This is their present stage in life. If they are willing to be helped, they can be helped. If they are willing to learn, if they are reasonably aware, they can learn to live more comfortably.

The vast majority of humans are functional, but laboring under misconceptions based on faulty understanding, or delusion. They are doing their best to fulfill their aspirations, and some of them are doing quite well. But often, among this large segment, major concerns have to do with personality-oriented desires and needs. They are involved in becoming more actualized, more successful, as human beings. Sincere thoughts of higher possibilities seldom enter their thinking for very long. If their religious impulses are expressed, they are often satisfied by a belief system, with concepts which provide a measure of emotional comfort and contain the hope of a future condition of true fulfillment, fulfillment which cannot be experienced now.

An increasing number of men and women, however, are actively thinking of higher possibilities, and many of them are also doing something about it. They are engaged in study, self-help strategies, achievement programs, and a variety of procedures with the hope of becoming more than they presently are—and perhaps all they can be. Some even aspire to total knowledge, to personal enlightenment.

I meet such people often because of the work that I do, and it is always a joy to work with individuals who are truly committed to a reasonable and useful course of action. Often, however, persons who affirm their commitment to learning and growing are not really committed yet. Instead, they want everything "their way." They will listen if what is said fits their rigid belief system. They will heed advice if they are not overly challenged. They will adhere to a program until a new or different one is made available to them. They say they want to be enlightened, but they do not even want to undergo the inner changes necessary for their psychological maturity.

To expect enlightenment without being willing to learn how to be a mature person is, with the rare exception of sudden conversion experience, too much to expect. Preparing ourselves by learning to live in a self-responsible way is almost inevitably a prerequisite to further spiritual unfoldment.

Proven Guidelines Supportive of our Spiritual Aspirations

There are specific things we can do to assist ourselves in the direction of awakening, growth, and fulfillment. These guidelines, while phrased variously in different enlightenment traditions, are common to them all, and one sentence includes them all: "The way to inner peace and harmony with nature is self-discipline, study and analysis of the life process, and transcending ego boundaries in order to experience the larger reality."

Self-discipline includes everything we intentionally do to resist and neutralize behavior which is destructive or which is not useful to final ends. Because any person who is still seeking will be contending with tendencies, drives, and habits which interfere with function and accomplishment, self-discipline is obviously needed. If we are resolved upon a course of action, we will be committed; and if we are committed, we will willingly enter into useful processes. This requires self-discipline—discipline in adjusting states of consciousness, discipline in matters of mental attitude and imagery, discipline of speech, discipline of moods and feelings, and disciplined behavior. We cannot merely read informative books, meditate for thirty minutes a day, and continue in an undisciplined manner if we expect to progress on the enlightenment path.

We may be attentive to useful practices for an hour or two a day, but what about the remaining hours? Are we allowing ourselves to be at the mercy of moods and circumstances the rest of the time? If we are sincere, we will welcome reasonable discipline, because it will afford us the opportunity to learn how to live a righteous life. With sufficient growth and maturity, we experience emotional balance, spontaneous clear consciousness, spontaneous right attitude and thinking, and spontaneous right behavior. But even if we want to do the right things all of the time, if undesirable inner tendencies and habits remain dominant, an orderly flow will be impeded.

Study and analysis of the life process includes inquiry into how and why the universe is as it is, what our real nature is, and what our relationship with the whole should be. An in-depth or even superficial study of diverse aspects of the material universe can help us function more freely and satisfy our natural curiosity, but even an exhaustive analysis of the relative realms will not satisfy the heart, the being. What is needed is an understanding of that which transcends the relative domain of manifest nature so that complete comprehension is achieved.

Some will be satisfied, for a while, with partial understanding. They may admit, "I really don't want to know everything right now. I just want to know enough to satisfy my mild desire to know, and to enable me to function as a human being with less pain and difficulty."

Some people actually begin their enlightenment quest because of a desire to remove pain and difficulty from their lives. Many begin their quest when they are ill and in need of healing or when they are emotionally distraught and in need of being restored to a degree of inner calm and balance. There are those, too, who seek knowledge in order to extend their influence and to more quickly achieve selfish goals. One thing is certain—any person who begins, for whatever reason, and who will persist will eventually learn the wisdom of righteous living and of surrendering egocentric drives to a higher influence. Healing can be experienced as a result of improving our relationship with the forces of nature. Emotional scars can be dissolved through right resolve and right effort. Even a person who seeks knowledge and power for selfish purposes will, in time, be "educated" by life itself and will learn the error of his ways.

Life is the great teacher. True, it is helpful to receive instruction from dependable sources. It is helpful to have a mentor, a true guru, to set an example and guide our steps. Through it all, however, it is the intelligence of life which is teaching us our lessons. Abide by certain laws and principles of nature, and we flourish. Disregard them or purposely go against them, and we experience the certain consequences.

Out of our states of consciousness (our levels of awareness), our mental states, and our general pattern of behavior unfold all of our circumstances. This is why it is important to learn how to be conscious, how to think clearly, and how to behave appropriately.

The reason a conscious understanding of and relationship with God is necessary is that the manifest universe is caused, supported, and nourished by God. The world is God's; it is not ours. We are life droplets in an ocean of consciousness, or like bubbles in the sea of life. All of the attributes and characteristics common to the Godhead are innate to us. Our role is to participate in harmonious ways in the creative processes of the universe, not to be self-serving because of the demands of the ego.

For our purposes let us define *ego* as the sense of individualized selfhood. So long as we do not know our true nature, so long as we feel ourselves to be separate from the ocean of life in which we live, we look out upon our world from the only perspective we have, that of an ego-bound personality. Actually, a degree of ego sense is useful to us so long as we are embodied. It would be difficult to pay attention to necessary matters in this world if we were consciously aware of being omnipresent, with the universe existing within our consciousness. (Many mystics, by the way, have reported that it is possible to experience such a reality during occasions of partial transcendence.)

What is needed is to allow the boundaries of ego

sense to partially dissolve so that we can retain self-sense while, at the same time, being in open communication with the world around us. By open communication I mean to acknowledge what is present to the senses while accepting into experience only that which is supportive. In this way we are able to experience what oneness is, what love is, what life is really about.

We often fear having our ego boundaries somewhat give way, exposing us to more open contact with our surroundings. We fear being vulnerable, of losing control, of not being the "us" we have become accustomed to being. At other times, when the episode is spontaneous and satisfying, for instance when we feel unconditional love for someone, or feel ourselves to be in perfect rapport with nature, we later confess that we wish we could feel like this always.

To assert, "I don't want to be enlightened if it means I have to renounce being me," is foolish, because it is based on lack of understanding of what enlightenment really is. With enlightenment, an increasing sense of cosmic awareness naturally occurs which is more satisfying, because it is more natural, than ego-structured consciousness could ever be.

Eventually, one who is devoted on the enlightenment path will experience that a higher power seems to be working through him and around him, as indeed it is. The power has always been present, and when we are more expansive, we are able to acknowledge it, and be thankful for it.

Among the guidelines frequently taught by enlightenment teachers are: harmlessness, truthfulness, honesty, right use of internal forces, and right understanding of our relationship with the material world.

Also taught are purity, serenity, and meditation leading to contemplation and transcendence of mental-emotional activities and sense-perceived objects which distract attention from the purpose of contemplation. Truthfulness, honesty, and a non-grasping relationship with the world enable us to be free from mental and emotional conflicts and to live in harmony with circumstances. Right use of internal forces means to use energies and inner resources wisely, for useful creative purposes, and to avoid wasting them. Energy can also be depleted from the body by stress, anxiety, worry, careless talk, and fruitless relationships and activities. When we are healthy and strong, and living correctly, some of the body's creative force is transmuted into finer essence which strengthens the immune system and contributes to increased vitality.

Purity refers to pure thoughts and motives, pure feelings about others and the world, and purification of the body, mental field, and nervous system. The body can be cleansed through natural means; the emotional nature through the practice of patience and serenity under all circumstances; and the mental field and nervous system through meditation and other therapeutic routines which will be discussed in a later chapter.

We should engage in the conscious experience of pure awareness, superconsciousness, through correct, regular meditation practice. During this interlude we will know our true nature, without the disturbing influences of sensory input, emotional unrest, or mental involvement. In "the temple of the undistracted mind," when even impulses that give rise to thought streams are stilled, we rest in the awareness of being, the supreme happiness.

Practice Session: Adjusting States of Consciousness at Will

Since our general patterns of experiences unfold from our states of consciousness and our habitual mental states, it is practical for us to become proficient in procedures which enable us to purposely adjust our states of consciousness. This shifting of awareness can be easily learned with patient and attentive practice. I will share a few procedures with you.

1. *Fall into Sleep and Awaken at Will*—You may already be skillful at this. Sleep is the state during which the body is restored and the nervous system partially rests. It is also the time when mental and emotional conflicts are resolved through dreams. Deep sleep, unconsciousness, is the absence of conscious or even partial awareness, although the sleeper, as a being, remains the witness to this state. After restful, dreamless sleep, you may admit that you "rested well." To sleep at will, turn within, relax, let thoughts recede, and go to sleep. To awaken at a predetermined time, decide to do so before you go to sleep, and you will awaken at the precise time decided upon. The *you* of you knows what time it is even when sleep is deep.

2. *Practice Conscious Sleep*—This may best be experienced at a time when you are not overly tired. Lie on your back, let the muscles of the body relax from the feet upward until you are aware only of being inside your skull. Feel yourself to be centered, perhaps at the heart center in the middle chest or at the space between the eyebrows, or both. Let yourself drift in the direction of sleep, observing the process carefully. With practice you will discover that point just between waking and

ordinary sleep, and will be able to remain there for a while. You can then contemplate your beingness, merely rest, or, should you dream lightly, be fully conscious of dream sequences. With practice you may even edit the dream, stop the action, learn to dream in color or in black and white at will. This state of conscious sleep can also be useful for the practice of creative imagination exercises, as well as for other interesting and creative purposes.

3. *Experience Superconsciousness at Will*—Superconsciousness, the state of clear non-mental awareness, is usually most easily experienced as a result of correct meditation practice. However, once you know from experience what the state is like, you may be able to assume it at will merely by releasing yourself from identification with feelings and thoughts. This is not a trance state or a hypnotic state, but a state of intense, clear awareness. It is the state of pure consciousness, awareness which is not diluted.

4. *View Your World with Detachment*—At times it is helpful to assume a detached attitude in order to objectively evaluate situations and circumstances. This is not the same as being averse to relating to the world or of wanting to withdraw from emotional involvement. Just practice, from time to time, looking upon your world as a passing drama. See events as transitional. See circumstances as effects of causes and subject to change. See clearly your own motives and the motives of others. Determine what your ideal relationship with your world would be and then relate to the world in that way. See clearly what your future circumstances should be and do what you need to do to allow them to unfold.

While doing these exercises, remain grounded in

the inner awareness of being. Do not overly indulge in fantasy or encourage hallucinations. Be intuitive, discerning, and rational. As a conscious being you should have command over your states of consciousness and your mental and emotional states.

One useful result of these exercises is help in realizing that we need not be restricted by habits, moods, or internal forces which may interfere with the free exercise of creative abilities. Few people know the extent to which they could express in useful ways if only they were not bound by habits and other conditionings. There is extensive literature reporting the unusual abilities of some people, with evidence to validate the stories. I have not seen anyone "fly through the air with the greatest of ease," but I have seen a holy man in India materialize objects in his hand through concentrated intention and the exercise of will. I have experienced out-of-body incidents and precognitive dreams, and I have witnessed circumstances unfold in accord with imaginal states.

The purpose of our practice now, however, is not to learn to do what others might feel to be extraordinary things, but rather to learn to do ordinary things extraordinarily well.

Be interested in all useful things, but avoid over-fascination with things which may distract you from the path of worthwhile growth and spiritual awareness.

Remember the basics and adhere to them. They will protect you from tempting diversions and contribute to balanced unfoldment. Avail yourself of the best study material available to ensure your spiritual and practical education. Cultivate the virtues, and live an ethical and moral life. Attend to your present duties and your given or chosen responsibilities with a cheerful attitude. Practice all needed disciplines and meditate daily. Yearn, with patience and faith, to know the whole truth about life. Live every moment of each day in the assurance that you are supported and nourished by the power that enlivens the universe—because you are.

Review

1. Relative aspects of nature are more comprehensible if we understand the absolute basis upon which all relative occurences manifest. Nature is supported by the field of pure consciousness.
2. From the field of pure consciousness, impulses arise which result in creative force, particles, and all of the components of nature.
3. When viewed subjectively, as the result of inner contemplation leading to insight, the universe is discerned as one thing, as a series of related aspects—a play of cosmic forces.
4. There is a "way of righteousness" pervading all of nature, and we can learn to be open to it and cooperate with it.
5. The inborn inclination of every person is to be able to fulfill all duties necessary to ensure the satisfaction of needs, to relate to the world harmoniously, and to achieve worthy purposes.
6. If we are resolved upon a course of action, we will be committed, and if we are committed, we will willingly enter into useful transformation processes.

7. So long as we do not know our true nature, so long as we feel ourselves to be separate from the ocean of life in which we live, we tend to look out upon our world as an ego-bound personality.

SELF-EVALUATION AND PLANNING

1. Agree within yourself to study the preceding chapter several times over the next few weeks.
2. In what areas of your life are you presently well disciplined?

3. In what areas of your life is more discipline required?

4. What will you do about it?

5. Every day, especially after quiet meditation, read from the scripture of your choice or from a useful inspirational source.
6. Practice the suggested techniques for adjusting states of consciousness. Notice your inner changes and your improved relationships.

If you throw your will on the side of victory, then the whole of the universe of reality throws itself behind your will, releases it, reinforces it, redeems it—and you.

—*E. Stanley Jones*

Blessed is the man that walketh not in the counsel of the ungodly...But his delight is in the law of the Lord; and in his law doth he meditate day and night. And he shall be like a tree planted by the rivers of water, that bringeth forth his fruit in his season; his leaf also shall not wither; and whatsoever he doeth shall prosper.

—*Psalms 1:1-3*

The vivid force of his mind prevailed, and he fared forth far beyond the flaming ramparts of the heavens and traversed the boundless universe in thought, and mind.

—*Lucretius*

CHAPTER 3

Awaken and Use the Creative Capacities of Your Mind

To correctly use the creative capacities of the mind we must understand its functions and integrate all of those capacities. The mind, understood and wisely used, enables us to fulfill worthy purposes easily. When mental functions are not understood and therefore not used wisely, conflicts, suffering, and pain can result.

The mind is not only capable of enabling us to actualize our desires and satisfy needs, it can also reflect the light of pure awareness, resulting in mental illumination and Self-realization.

While engaging in the study and wise use of our mental capacities, let us remember that we are spiritual beings and that the mind is merely a perceptual mechanism through which we relate to the world in which we live. The mind is designed to process information, standing between us and the external environment. We receive information about our environment when it is transmitted through the senses and nerves to the brain, the organ of the mind. There data is received and processed. A considerable quantity of information received by the brain is automatically processed by the lower brain, which regulates involuntary body processes such as temperature, respiration, hormonal secretions, blood circulation, and various other body-survival activities. All information received by the mind is stored at the subconscious level, even if it is not consciously acknowledged, thus adding to the storehouse of memory.

The Four Major Functions of the Mental Field

Our minds are really fields which are particularizations of a cosmic mental field. Because of this we are able to influence the outer environment with our mental images and will. We share a common mind, cosmic mind, and the mind we know as our own is bounded by our individual self-consciousness, or sense of individual selfhood. The first function of our mind, then, is to enable us to maintain this sense of individual existence, or ego sense. Remember, however, it is possible to extend personal awareness beyond the boundaries usually accepted and to have access to the entire range of cosmic mind. It is also possible to transcend cosmic mind and experience pure existence, which we do during moments of spontaneous transcendence and during occasions of profound meditation.

The second function of the mental field is to be the repository of feelings and memory. Our awareness pervades the entire mental field, whether we are conscious of it or not. During subconscious states, we often have access to memory and we are conscious of dreaming. During unconscious states, we are not alert enough to clearly discern the contents of the mental field, yet at unconscious levels the accumulated impressions of all we have thought, felt, or perceived are stored. Many of the tendencies and drives which determine to some extent our thinking and behavior are rooted at this level.

The third function of the mental field is that of thinking, the processing of information; and this function is what we often think of as the definition of what the human mind is. But there is a fourth function—the faculty of intelligence—which enables us to examine information presented to the mind and to discern what is to be known about it.

The subjective side of intelligence is intuition, the faculty of direct knowing. It is by using intelligence and intuition that we are able to examine extremely subtle, and fine, subjects and acquire understanding and insight through revelation.

As mental faculties are integrated and personal awareness increases, intellectual powers increase, as well as the ability to use intuition to know things which cannot be known through mental processes alone. The being which uses the mental field is, after all, superior to it and has within itself the knowledge of consciousness, as well as the ability to comprehend any aspect of relative manifestation of consciousness.

Faulty perception creates confusion in the mind, leading to conflicts and errors in judgment. The major error in perception is that of falsely assuming oneself to be a mind or a mind/body organism. Another major error which follows is that of believing that external circumstances can unduly influence or control us. With spiritual awakening, one realizes his relationship with mental faculties and the body, and his relationship with the environment in which he lives. He then knows that he can, if he is willing to do so, live as a self-determined being rather than as a victim of either internal drives and tendencies or outer circumstances. When consciousness is liberated as a result of true understanding, one can then live freely in a supportive and responsive universe, inwardly happy all of the time, while also experiencing the enjoyment and satisfaction which accompany successful creative activities and relationships. One of the results of being grounded in true inner happiness is that life can be experienced in completely natural ways, rather than our having to withdraw permanently from relationships in order to preserve inner peace.

A variety of factors can contribute to faulty or incomplete perception when we are not fully aware or not functional because of inner conflicts, or when neurological or biological impairment exists. When we are preoccupied, worried, daydreaming, introverted, or otherwise not paying attention, we simply do not see what is present in our environment to be observed, or do we fully comprehend the signals others may attempt to convey to us.

Discernment may be lacking even when we try to understand, so we are able to comprehend only a portion of what we are trying to understand. If we have strong opinions about what is so, we will hear only what we want to hear and ignore the rest of the information—information which could be useful for us to consider and reflect upon. People who are narrow-minded and opinionated almost always disregard information which does not match their preconceived notions of what is true, important, or useful. Some people have difficulty comprehending what they read but are able to process information if they hear it; the reverse is true for others. Extreme tiredness or stress can interfere with our ability to correctly perceive what the senses present to us. An imbalance of blood chemistry can contribute to errors in perception. The presence of drugs in the system almost always interferes with the processing of information. Attitude can interfere with perception, so that if we believe we are incapable of comprehending, we will find it difficult to do so.

We see our world from our own points of view. Depending upon how our "inner world" is, so will we tend to see the world around us. When we are pessimistic, moody, or withdrawn, or if we feel incompetent or victims of circumstances, we will tend to see about us only that which reinforces our present states of consciousness and mental attitudes. When we are optimistic, happy, in good rapport with our environment, and enthusiastic about possibilities, we will be inclined to see about us opportunities to learn, to grow, and to excel.

Your inner world, the world as you have it imaged in your mind, is not exactly the same world as anyone else's. When the pictures in your mind, and the assumptions you have made, approximate those of others whom you meet, you may conclude that you have found a new friend because of a mutual understanding of what life is like and what living should be like. You tend to see and hear those things which reinforce your

personal world-view, the preconceived images you
have about how life should be for you, or can be for
you. If your inner picture of what life is like is limited,
you will see limitation. If your inner realization is that
of expansion, growth, and achievement, you will see
opportunities for expansion, growth, and achievement.
We seldom see the world as it is. We usually see it as we
presume it to be.

How do you presently see your world? Can you
choose to see it differently? Do you like the world you
presently see, or would you prefer to see it another
way? Do you see limitation, chaos, struggle, sickness,
and evil everywhere? Or can you see instead unlimited
opportunity, order, progressive growth, wellness, and
goodness everywhere? The only difference between
"saints" and those who are not yet manifesting higher
qualities and virtues is the difference between seeing
life as it really is versus seeing it from a distorted point
of view.

An important thing to remember is that, if we are
reasonably healthy-minded, we can choose to look
upon the world as we decide. We can choose our states
of consciousness, our mental attitudes, and how clearly
we will perceive what the world presents to us. And if
usual states of consciousness and mental states are not
what we would like them to be because of habit, we can
change our habits of feeling, thinking, and behavior to
actually become the kind of people we want to be. To
do this we have to accept personal responsibility for
doing these things—we have to decide to be mature
persons. It may not always be as easy as we initially
think it might be to be mature, because of mental confusion, emotional conflicts, and environmental factors we

have learned to adapt to; but with willingness, and practice, we can unfold and accomplish our purposes.

What is Most Important to You Right Now?

Right now, before you have time to think about the matter, what is the most important thing, relationship, or possibility in your life? What do you live to do? What motivates you to do most of the things you do?

A suggestion here: write down your thoughts and describe your present feelings about your relationship to life as you presently experience it, and what you see for your future from where you presently are.

Our dominant thoughts and feelings, as well as our habitual behavior, are a fairly accurate indication of what we presently consider to be important to us. Thoughts and feelings determine behavior, and our behavior, our patterns of living, is what our lives are. Even if certain needs or wants are deepseated, below the threshold of conscious awareness, they are strongly influential in determining our behavior.

It may be that you are not doing the things you really, deep down, want to do, but are spending most of your time and energy in coping, surviving, fulfilling the expectations of others, or waiting for that eventual day when you will finally settle into the real purpose for being in this world. In the meantime, by doing your best while involved with present activities you will be preparing yourself to function more effectively when your real purpose is known and your life has positive direction.

It may be that you are already on course, already clearly involved with processes leading to meaningful accomplishment. If so, continue as you are, while being open to discovery, to learning, to awakening more to possibilities. An inner indication that you are on the right course is if you are creatively involved with no disturbance of inner happiness. Remember, inner happiness does not mean complacency—it means that you are centered in being, in your true Self, and from this center you function creatively to accomplish whatever you are inspired to accomplish.

To achieve worthy goals, to accomplish useful purposes, to expand more and more in the direction of cosmic awareness, and to make helpful contributions to society and Planet Earth—these are some of the reasons we are involved with the life process. A human being is an innovator, a goal-achiever, a problem-solver; and all of these things, and more, can be accomplished joyfully, without undue stress or strain. Our inner happiness should be evident in our lives and revealed in the things we do. When we know inner happiness, joy will bubble to the surface and radiate into the environment, touching others and bringing forth their inner happiness.

Four Basic Ways to Accomplish Purposes

There are four basic ways to accomplish worthy purposes. They will usually be mingled, with one way being dominant. Often, until we are stable in performing from the level of understanding which makes the most useful way possible, we will move from one way to another. Consider this a learning process.

The Way of Most Effort. This is the way of doing the best we can with limited understanding of the laws of creative achievement. At this level we work hard, exchanging our personal effort and time for results expected, the way of physical activity. There is nothing dishonorable about this way and there are times when it is the only way to get a job done. But it is restrictive to the ideal of major accomplishment, because we can only do so much in a given time. In a given time period we can only type so many words, hammer so many nails, shovel so much dirt, drive so many miles, make so many telephone calls, prepare so much food—in short, what we can accomplish is limited by our performance capacity at any given task. We are here talking about productivity, not about quality, although quality work should be an ideal even when performing at this level. Then, there are quality things we can be doing which do require time and patient, attentive effort. When personal needs are met, and they should be met easily, we are free to use our talents and resources in more creatively satisfying ways.

The Way of Less Effort. This is the way of innovation, the way of planning with clear vision, the way of harnessing the energy of machines and other labor-saving devices. This is also the way of cooperative effort, utilizing the combined talents and energies of several people who share common purposes. Very useful at this level is the ability to be clear in your mind about what is important and what is not important, what is result-producing and what is not. Here we come to understand the importance of establishing priorities. Merely by eliminating those things from your life which are not useful to ultimate ends, and by focusing on those things which can assist you to more quickly accomplish your purposes, stress is reduced, errors are minimized, and goals are achieved more easily.

The Way of Least Effort. Many already function this
way naturally. It is the way of using possibility-thinking and imagination to plan end results and visualize
them so clearly that every thought, feeling, and action
we have follows naturally to enable us to realize our
desired ends. Note that I did not say "accomplish" our
desired ends. This is because when we work from the
level of possibility-thinking and imagination, we attract to ourselves circumstances, people, and resources
which make possible the fulfillment of our imagined
dreams. So it is not we who are doing it all; we are instead learning to work with the responsive forces of nature which, by their very character, tend to flow into
manifestation according to the mental pattern presented to them. You may have functioned naturally this
way all of your life and be wondering why the matter is
being mentioned here. I am explaining it because many
people, sincerely doing their best to be successful in
current ventures, have not heard of the process or, if
they have heard of it, have not yet learned to use it effectively.

The Way of No Effort. This is the way of grace, the
way of spontaneous right action and orderly unfoldment which occurs when we are in our right place in
the universe, doing what we should be doing in line
with personal soul destiny, and open to the guidance
and support of the evolutionary trends in nature. One
experiencing this level of activity may appear to do
very little to cause effects, or he may be very busy keeping appointments and playing his role in the creative
process, but he is always conscious that he is not making anything happen, that he is going along with the
flow. Sometimes when working from this level, a per-

son may have to still think of priorities and be innovative in order to handle the many opportunities presented by life. One will often need to be self-reminded to attend to personal routines, including meditation and rest periods, to avoid becoming too caught up in projects and activities. We are not the sole agents through whom grace can flow, so we should realize that others can also be participants in the game of life.

Possibility Thinking, Controlled Mental Imagery, and Follow-Through

I explained earlier the necessity of being moral, ethical, and self-responsible, so please understand that the procedures here offered are for the purpose of enabling you to unfold your latent abilities, expand consciousness, and experience more fully the kind of life you are meant to experience. Because these procedures are impersonal principles, they are result-producing for anyone; but if motives are not pure because of psychological conflicts or errors in perception, final results will not be satisfying for the person who uses them or for others who might be involved. If our motives are not pure, we cannot be in harmony with the purposes of evolution. Harmony, right action, personal enlightenment, social health, and planetary wellness are in line with evolutionary purposes. Included in harmony and right action are the meeting of all basic needs and the satisfaction of natural desires.

Possibility-thinking, controlled imagination, and follow-through come under the category of *the way of least effort* and prepare one for *the way of no effort*. Using the procedures now under examination, we are able to learn to work cooperatively with cosmic mind. We are doing this anyway, even when unaware of the fact and when thinking and feelings are undisciplined. The thoughts we think and the feelings we have about our status in life reflect as behavior and circumstances. Most influential of all is our awareness of being. If we are aware of ourselves as spiritual beings, we will function from this understanding. If we assume ourselves to be something else, we will think and behave accordingly. The only difference between individuals and their circumstances is their states of consciousness and mental states. What I feel to be true of myself is what I am currently expressing in my life. What you feel to be true of yourself is what you are currently expressing in your life.

The solutions to all human problems are within the state of consciousness, the awareness of being, of every person. While it is true that random changes in outer circumstances can contribute to shifts in consciousness and feelings of wellbeing, or otherwise, the major determining factor is within us. How we determine to be, to think, to image, and to function is the major factor in how we relate to our world and what we experience.

If I know myself to be a spiritual being, superior to thoughts, feelings, and external circumstances, my world will unfold about me according to my inner knowing. If I assume myself to be anything other than a spiritual being, whatever I assume I am is what I will experience. Our personal assumptions determine how we view our world and how we relate to it. If desirable changes are to take place in our lives we must inwardly agree to learning those procedures which will result in self-mastery, mastery of our states of consciousness.

From these proceed everything else. Rich or poor, happy or unhappy, healthy or ill, successful or not successful, these conditions have their cause within our own consciousness, our awareness of who we are.

If misunderstanding is present, if mental confusion and emotional conflicts are dominant, we may not be able to feel comfortable about being prosperous, healthy, and successful. We will then, usually at subconscious levels, contrive to prevent the very fulfillment we may consciously assert that we desire. Do not be cynical and say that these procedures do not work. If you are not able to use them effectively, be honest about the fact that your understanding is not yet perfect or that you have not completely entered into the processes which can result in needed transformation, awakening, and desired results.

Even when we know about these procedures, we may not use them because of some inner resistance to change. This is why I now encourage you to apply all of the principles here shared and to enter into every process until you acquire proficiency through personal practice. This is the only way to ensure your spiritual education and to unfold your inborn capacities.

Possibility Thinking. Use the note pages in this book, as well as a personal notebook, to enter into regular possibility thinking sessions. During a quiet interlude, relax, meditate a few minutes, and open yourself to creative ideas as they surface in your mind. As they do, jot them down, even the ones which at first seem extreme or impractical. You can cross them out later if you want to. Think of improvements you would like to see unfold in your life, in every area: spiritual, mental, emotional, physically, in your relationships, and in worthy projects and ventures. Follow the suggested outline in the forms provided at the end of this chapter. You will be doing one of the most useful things possible to clearly see yourself in relationship to your world, to establish priorities, dream noble dreams, solve problems, and live in harmony with energies and circumstances around you.

As you do this, think of your personal destiny as a spiritual being. Why are you in this world? Are you doing what you should be doing? Are you living the kind of life you should be living? Be absolutely fearless as you do this, and inwardly feel that you are in partnership with the Higher Power, because you are. Life wants you to be fulfilled, to thrive, to flourish, to prosper in all ways. When you are thriving, when you are flourishing, when you are prospering in all ways, you can better assist others to do these things.

Controlled Mental Imagery. After engaging in possibility thinking for a while, proceed to the next phase, that of consciously regulating mental imagery through creative visualization. When you engage in possibility thinking, which is very important, you may tend to become involved at the level of fantasy or wishful thinking. This is why we move on to consciously regulating mental states and feeling states, in relationship to our reasonable goals. Remember, "what I am" determines my attitude, thoughts and feelings. So first, meditate more deeply until you feel yourself to be clear, aware and peaceful, until you can feel that all things are possible. When you do this you remove your awareness from restrictive thoughts and feelings, and rest in the awareness of self-completeness, self-sufficiency, and competence.

Now, visualize a mental scene which implies the fulfillment of your agreed-upon worthy desire. If you want to be more spiritually aware, visualize how life would be for you if this were so. If you want to be more mentally clear and able, visualize how life would be if this were so. Do the same thing with all areas of your life—emotional, physical, in matters of relationships, and the fulfillment of worthy projects of any kind.

When you are firmly established in the mental state, arouse your feelings and feel yourself fulfilled in relationship to that envisioned circumstance. At this time do not concern yourself with how this can come to pass, but just live in the feeling of the desire fulfilled. Feel it to be a *now* reality, not a future possibility.

You may choose to inwardly see and feel yourself to be totally fulfilled in all areas of personal experience. Or you may focus on just one area, or one project. This is a matter of preference, but I find it better to be all-inclusive.

Once settled in the inner conviction of being the person you want to be and feeling the feelings you want to feel, remain in this state for as long as comfortable, until you feel yourself firmly established in it.

Now you are no longer the person you were before you began the process. You are more conscious, more aware, more confident, more mentally clear, more emotionally centered, more comfortable with your relationships, and confident about future unfoldments in your life.

Follow Through. This is important—do not revert to your former state of consciousness and feeling-state. Remain firmly settled in the new state of consciousness, with corresponding feelings and with an open mind and a trusting heart. That is, be established in faith, for faith is the substance of hope, the inner evidence of that which will surely unfold on the screen of space-time.

Now that you are the person you have chosen to be, the person you should be, whatever thoughts you think, feelings you feel, and actions you perform will unfold from your present state of consciousness. Circumstances will unfold to correspond to your state of consciousness; problems will be solved, opportunities will be forthcoming, the world will appear brighter to you, and you will be in the flow of endless good. This is why this process naturally leads to the fourth, effortless way of fulfilling purposes; it opens you to the supportive influences of life which are always benevolent.

You do not have to speculate about the usefulness of these processes or discuss them with persons who are not open to possibilities. You have only to enter into your practice alone. What you do in private will reflect outwardly. Instead of wasting time and energy in idle talk and purposeless action, use these procedures. Out of your inner happiness will flow satisfying relationships and circumstances. This is the inner way to the actualization, the making real, of worthy dreams—and it never fails.

How to Correctly use Constructive Affirmations

By the words we speak we reveal ourselves to ourselves and to others. Our habitual trend of conversation accurately reflects our awareness of being and our mental and emotional states. Also, when we intentionally regulate our speech we are able to regulate feelings, mental states, and states of consciousness.

Therefore, at all times, even during relaxed occasions of social interaction, speak with intention and allow yourself to say only those words which are positive, constructive, and useful.

Even casual conversation can be constructive, instead of destructive or purposeless. For instance, we can say, "It's good to see you," instead of, "How are you?" Or, "Isn't it a beautiful day?" instead of, "Isn't it a terrible world?" We can choose to remain silent when others speak in negative ways, then steer the conversation to more useful subjects. The most important thing is your inner awareness of being, and your feeling of confidence and contentment. When these are settled, you can mingle in any social situation and get along easily.

Now and then, during the course of the average day, you may feel the need to center yourself and to adjust your mental attitude and emotional state. For this, use constructive affirmation. Just think of a phrase which is a declaration of the state of consciousness you want to experience, and speak it aloud to yourself. If others are present, speak it inwardly, with realization.

For instance, "I am a spiritual being, firmly grounded in the ocean of divine consciousness. I am calm, confident, and efficient. I am happy, I am joyful, I am thankful." Use words which are natural and comfortable to you.

Speak them aloud at first, if convenient, naturally and with conviction; then quietly, then at a whisper, then mentally; then *feel* the reality of the statement. This is the sequence: aloud, quietly, whisper, mentally, then *feeling.* In this way you move in successive stages from the beginning to the conclusion, the realization of that which is the embodiment of the affirmation.

While subconscious patterns will be affected by correct use of affirmations, as well as creative visualization, our basic intent is not to engage in any conditioning of the subconscious level of the mind. We are primarily interested in adjusting the state of consciousness, to be established in the awareness of being which naturally results in all other needed adjustments on mental and emotional levels. So do not struggle to force the subconscious to accept your conscious efforts; simply engage in these processes in a relaxed, accepting manner, and results will be forthcoming.

Always cultivate optimism, cheerfulness, confidence, love, faith in life, and positive expectancy. These attitudes are health-producing, will strengthen the immune system, and encourage balance between mind, feelings, and body. Attitudes of pessimism, depression, anxiety, fear, and distrust contribute to disturbing internal harmony, weaken the immune system, and cause errors in perception and judgment.

Use These Methods to Heal and Regulate Any Condition

Use controlled visualization and affirmation to restore order in your life and to heal and regulate any condition. The major causes of personal problems are faulty perception of circumstances and what we project upon our environment through imagination and expectancy. All too often we feel we are victims of inner influences and outer circumstances, when upon closer, honest examination, we must conclude that we ourselves are playing a major role in creating and maintaining the circumstances in our lives. Once we understand this, we can choose to change the way we look at the world and the way we think about circumstances, and then initiate purposeful causes which will result in desired effects.

If you are in need of healing of any kind, learn what you must do to release the healing forces within you. If you need the help of a trained physician or therapist, seek out the right person who thinks and practices holistically and get the help you need. You can be helped, but you will have to be responsible for maintaining a program which is useful. In other words, the healing will occur because of what you do, not because of what is done to you or for you.

Start by inwardly seeing yourself well in every way. The healing process will begin. You may be led to the right source of assistance, or to helpful information, and the intelligence within you and around you will work with you if you do your part.

We will deal more with healing in a later chapter. Just remember that the power within you, which is also nourishing the universe, can assist you in the direction of wholeness and the completion of all worthy purposes.

Review

1. To correctly use the creative capacities of the mind, you must understand and integrate its functions.

2. Faulty perception creates confusion in the mind, leading to conflicts and errors in judgement.
3. We can choose our states of consciousness, our mental attitudes, and how clearly we will perceive the world around us.
4. If you are already on course, already clearly involved with processes leading to meaningful accomplishment, continue as you are—while being open to discovery, to learning, to awakening more and more to possibilities.
5. Review the basic ways of accomplishing worthy purposes—the way of most effort, the way of less effort, the way of least effort, and the way of no effort.
6. Review the process of using possibility thinking and creative imagery, and practice what you learn.
7. Practice using affirmations.
8. The power within you, which nourishes the universe, can assist you in the direction of wholeness and the completion of all worthy purposes.

SELF-EVALUATION AND PLANNING

1. Write a short paragraph describing the four functions of the mental field.

2. How does your "inner world" differ from that of some of the people you know?

3. Right now, what is the most important thing in life for you?

4. Write your thoughts and feelings about your present relationship to life and what you see for your future from your present point of view.

5. Write a list of your hopes and dreams, for yourself and for others.

I salute the supreme teacher, the Truth whose nature is bliss, who is the giver of the highest happiness, who is pure wisdom, who is beyond all qualities and infinite like the sky, who is beyond words, who is one and eternal, pure and still, who is beyond all change and phenomena and who is the silent witness to all our thoughts and emotions. I salute Truth, the supreme teacher.

—*Vedic Hymn*

After a person has attained the highest perfection while in the body, he can attain the Supreme Vision. With pure understanding and controlled thoughts and actions, keeping his own counsel, being moderate in all things and practicing deep meditation, removing from his consciousness everything that is not God-like, such a person becomes purified and knows the Ultimate Truth.

—*Bhagavad Gita*

When you pray, say, Our Father which art in heaven, hallowed be thy name, Thy kingdom come, Thy will be done, as in heaven, so in earth.

—*Luke 11:2*

CHAPTER 4

Meditate Like This for Positive Results

Whether only for the immediate benefits which can result, or also for spiritual growth, every person who wants life enhancement should meditate. It is also the one sure way to experience inner self-completeness, the basis of forever happiness.

Meditation is the simple process of turning attention, and internal forces, back to their source. It is done consciously so that internal changes are observed and experienced and attention flows through mental levels smoothly and easily until a clear, undistracted state of consciousness is experienced. This state of consciousness, being unrelated to feelings and thoughts, is known as *superconsciousness*—to contrast it with states of consciousness and mental states usually known during waking and sleep.

Do not confuse the meditation process with any form of auto-conditioning or self-suggestion, for since

it results in transcendence of mental states, it has no relationship to mental conditioning processes.

Until it is experienced the actual process of meditation must remain a mystery to the uninitiated, because
superconsciousness, being a pure state of awareness,
cannot be related to lower mind activities.
Any reasonably intelligent person who is willing
to learn to meditate can be taught to do so in a very
short time. Meditation is useful for people of all ages in
all walks of life. It is for those interested in improved
mental and physical function as well as for those inclined in the direction of total self-understanding.

What Happens When We Meditate

To acquire some understanding of why meditation is
effective, let us examine what occurs during the process. Ordinarily, during normal states of consciousness,
our awareness is influenced by sensory impressions,
emotions, and mental processes, so that the average
person seldom has the opportunity to experience clear
awareness. Also, environmental concerns may cause us
to be almost forever thinking about relating, coping,
and accomplishing our purposes. Seldom does one really experience total relief from the many demands
made upon his time and resources. Stress accumulates,
emotions become unsettled, thoughts become confused, relationships become disturbed, priorities are
often neglected or forgotten. Regular daily meditation,
correctly practiced, can make a major beneficial difference in our lives, because during meditation we have
the opportunity to temporarily withdraw from all that

challenges and disturbs, thus experiencing conscious, restful awareness.

As we sit with closed eyes in a quiet environment, directing the attention inward, emotions and mental processes become less agitated, due to diminished sensory input. As the breathing rhythm slows, because of diminished oxygen needs and because the body is still, emotions begin to subside and thought processes become more orderly. Brain wave patterns tend to become synchronized. Eventually, the impulses from the unconscious which contribute to stirring thought processes diminish in intensity, resulting in a calm mental state. Through it all the meditator is both the observer and the experiencer. There is little chance, then, of becoming passive or involved with fantasy.

It is possible, of course, to drift into a passive state and become involved with drifting mental processes, but not if you adhere to meditation practice as here taught. If you are not willing to learn to meditate correctly, and to maintain correct procedures, there is no point in getting involved with the process in the first place. Even if you persist in passive states of consciousness instead of meditating correctly, there would be no harm done, but such involvement would be merely a waste of time and the real purpose for meditating would be neglected. Meditation, then, is obviously for persons who are sincere about accomplishing their purposes and who want to unfold their inborn capacities so that life can be lived as it is meant to be lived.

As oxygen needs are diminished and the blood is cleansed of carbon dioxide (because of natural breathing in a relaxed state), breathing becomes slower and slower. No attempt at breath regulation is necessary, as this is an entirely natural occurrence. Vital forces in the body become harmonized, contributing to deep relaxation and reduction in stress. As stress is reduced, mental and physical processes begin to function as they were designed to function. Body systems tend to be restored to orderly function, and the immune system is strengthened. Actual chemical changes occur in the body during meditation which are conducive to wellness.

As emotions settle and thought activity becomes more orderly, concentration becomes easy and the meditator can then direct his attention at will, without effort.

A meditator usually directs attention to the higher brain centers, at least in the early stages, because this helps to withdraw attention from the senses and from body-related sensations. Also, since the higher brain centers are the ones through which clearer states of consciousness are processed, it makes sense to purposely direct the attention there. In other words, we want to detach attention from sense objects, from body sensations, from emotions, and from mental activity in order to experience transcendence. This is done without effort, without the use of will power. It is done with gentle intention, without anxiety for results. Results are automatic and spontaneous when meditation is practiced correctly.

To maintain a steady inward flow of attention, certain procedures are recommended which are enjoyable and effective. I will explain a few of them as we proceed. With deep relaxation and settling of emotions and thought activity, the attention remains internalized. Real meditation can then be experienced. The natural result of sustained introversion is, sooner or later, the peak experience for that meditation session, or states of consciousness very near to it.

Ideally, you will experience the clear state every time you meditate. One reason for this is that this state of consciousness is the goal of meditation and results in the many benefits which can be experienced. The other reason is that if success is not experienced during meditation, the meditator may begin to notice inner resistance to the meditation process. After all, we do not really like to do things which are not going to be successful.

This is a simple explanation of the psycho-physiological (spirit-mind-body) basis of meditation. It is not complicated, it is fairly easy to understand, and it is entirely natural. Now and then I meet a person who admits to some uncertainty about learning to meditate. The anxiety may be due to the mistaken belief that meditation will somehow result in peculiar mental or emotional changes, or that one may become involved with interior situations which cannot be understood or handled. For a rational person such fears are groundless. Irrational people should not be taught to meditate anyway, but should be assisted in the direction of mental and emotional wellness first. A sometimes contributing factor to resistance to meditation is the not-so-hidden underlying fear that meditation *will* result in changes, changes which a problem-centered person may really not want to occur. A small percentage of the human population, for one reason or another, prefer to remain ignorant and provincial. Meditation is for persons who are willing to be self-responsible and who are open to growth and fulfillment.

Observed Benefits of Correct Meditation Practice

The benefits resulting from correct meditation practice have been widely observed and reported. A few such benefits are stress reduction, orderly thought activity, emotional calm, strengthening of the body's immune system, improvement in general function of all internal systems, improvement in intellectual capacity, improved powers of memory, awakened intuitive abilities, and retardation of biological aging processes. These benefits are not only reported by meditators themselves, but have been observed by researchers who have carefully monitored the body chemistry, behavior, and personality changes of meditators.

Stress is naturally reduced in the body when attention is withdrawn from externals and when breathing rhythms are ideal. Anxiety is diminished, and emotions and mental processes are no longer agitated. Stress accumulation in the body interferes with normal functioning of the body's major systems, contributing to high blood pressure and disturbances of the flow of nerve impulses. Emotions are influenced adversely, thought processes are confused, and intellectual powers are veiled. Too much stress results in a lowering of the body's immune system, allowing illness to occur. Meditation can assist in the reduction of stress, but you must also learn to cultivate constructive mental attitudes and emotional states to be able to live in the world without becoming overstressed.

One reason for the slowing of aging processes is that during meditation, and afterwards, body systems are cooled and internal processes are slowed. Mild body temperature lowering has been observed in meditators during practice sessions.

The most dramatic result of sustained meditation practice is an increase in spiritual awareness. The meditator discovers that his or her real nature is consciousness, quite apart from mental processes, feelings, and body functions. During meditation you have the opportunity to actually experience beingness, pure awareness without thoughts or emotions. You then know for certain that spirit is other than mind or body, even while related to them for the purpose of expression in this world. This personal discovery can change your entire outlook and result in your coming to terms with the world in a realistic way, seeing differently and thus acquiring a clearer understanding of what life's purpose is.

Meditators reportedly tend to be healthier, more mentally and emotionally stable, more successful in ventures, and more able to relate to friends and associates effectively. High school and college students develop better study habits, and their grade averages improve if they meditate regularly. Job performance is better and errors are fewer among office and factory workers who meditate. In short, no matter the profession or life style of a person who meditates, because of awakened consciousness and improved overall function, life is enhanced in every way.

Scheduling Your Meditation Practice

Twice a day is the recommended schedule for meditation practice. Many people meditate once a day and find this to be satisfactory for them. Suitable times are early in the morning before beginning the day's activities, and in the evening when the work day is over. In the morning, after restful sleep and before thoughts and moods have become involved with duties, is a good time for meditation because it is easier then to remain inwardly settled and to contemplate. For this reason many arrange to awaken sooner than usual to allow time for body-cleansing routines and meditation. In the evening, meditation can help to reduce any stress which has built up during the day. If neither morning nor evening meditation is convenient, any convenient time will do.

To provide every opportunity for success in meditation, you will want to ensure a quiet place where there is no possibility of disturbance. You will also want to allow at least thirty minutes for practice, and longer if you intend to follow through with intentional creative work of some kind, such as contemplating solutions to problems, acquiring insights into any aspect of life, goal setting, prayer for others, and so on. Shorter meditations are suitable for stress reduction and centering, while longer sessions are useful for deeper work.

You may want to provide a regular place for meditation—a secluded room or a special place which is yours alone for your inner work. The important thing is to plan with intention and then follow through on a regular schedule.

Beginning meditators should plan to meditate regularly for at least six weeks to allow time for proficiency to be developed and for definite changes to occur. Results are often immediate, but it is better to be committed to a reasonable schedule of practice. Short term and long term commitment is evidence of self-responsibility.

Meditation is to be practiced, not overly discussed with others. Of course, talking with an experienced meditator in order to learn the fine points of practice is useful, but to superficially talk about the process or one's personal experiences is not useful. Too much casual conversation about anything that is important reveals our lack of sincere purpose.

Having helpful instruction sources, such as this book, to help you understand the meditation process and for inspiration can also be useful. Before starting your practice be sure you are completely and correctly informed about how to proceed.

How to Meditate

Approach your practice session in a relaxed frame of mind. Anticipate the meditation session and expect it to be satisfying. Don't expect specific results; rather, let results unfold naturally, as they will.

1. *Posture*—Sit upright in a comfortable chair, with your spine straight and head erect. Close your eyes and let your inner gaze flow to the space between your eyebrows. Do not strain as you do this. Be gentle with yourself. Inhale and exhale rather deeply a few times, but don't overdo it. Breathing should be natural and easy, from the diaphragm, without obvious physical effort. Breathe in peace and calm, and breathe out stress and tension.

2. *Focus and Technique*—Do not struggle to control your thoughts or feelings. Ignore them. Look within, knowing that behind your thoughts and feelings is the clear field of pure consciousness you will experience. If you are devotional by nature, think of God and of your

relationship with God. Surrender to the process. Surrender to the goodness of life, within you and around you.

It may be that all you then need to do is sit in the silence, looking gently within, listening gently within, and being open to discovery. Meditation may occur spontaneously, as inner forces ascend the spinal pathway to the higher brain.

If this does not occur easily, introduce a technique into the process. As you breathe in, let a word of your choice float in your mind. Just "listen" to it in your mind. It may be the word *peace,* or *joy,* or *God.* As you breathe out, let the word again float in your mind. This is an easy way to proceed. The attractive "word sound" of your choice will be your mantra, the sound which fascinates your attention and attracts it inward without effort.

You can still be aware of feelings and thoughts as you proceed, but they will be in the background. Gradually, as your attention is more and more absorbed in the process and the inner "word sound," you will be oblivious to thoughts or feelings, and they will settle of their own accord.

3. *Continue to Meditate*—Continue in this manner until you are peaceful, calm, and content. Even the conscious use of the technique will be forgotten as you become established in the awareness of conscious, clear being. Here rest, for as long as comfortable. This is the most useful and therapeutic phase of practice.

4. *Conclude the Practice Session*—When you feel inclined, conclude the practice session by returning to mind-feeling-body awareness. Open your eyes and sit for a few moments to experience the calm after-effects of meditation, then go about your next scheduled routine or program.

For many, prayer is the most effective prelude to meditation. You simply inwardly talk with God until you experience a feeling of attunement; then sit in the silence, waiting with mild expectancy. Again sit upright with your inner gaze directed to the space between your eyebrows and with attention in the higher brain.

A mantra is a sound formula which allows attention to flow to a chosen point of focus so that it does not remain involved with feelings and thought patterns. Many meditation traditions teach a form of mantra meditation, because it is easy for almost anyone to practice and it is result-producing. The benefits of mantra meditation are most obvious when one follows the procedure as given, without straining to force results.

With practice, if you will listen in the inner ear, you will discern a sound, or a medley of sounds. In this way you discover that you have your own mantra within you, available to be listened to at any time. Listen to the naturally occurring sound. Feel yourself somewhat dissolving in the sound. Know that the sound you hear is an aspect of the primal sound of creative force pervading the universe. Know that behind the sound or sounds you initially hear are subtle sounds, and behind them are finer sounds. Behind fine sounds is soundlessness, the pure field of being.

The initial sounds heard in the inner ear are gross sounds created by movement of air in the ear canal. Next you can hear subtle sounds, which are the varying frequencies of the body's electrical currents. Finer sounds can then be discerned, resulting in the perception of a clear sound. Since during the meditation process the ideal is to experience a shift of attention from the outer to the inner, from gross perceptions to awareness of the clear field of consciousness, following the inner sound to the source of sound is a practical way to proceed. Once you are settled in the practice of listening to internal sound, all other distractions having been minimized, the inward flowing of attention is steady and spontaneous.

Sitting in a darkened room, listening to the inner sound and gazing at the space between the eyebrows, the place known to yogis as the spiritual eye, you may perceive inner light. At first you may perceive mental phenomena—dream-like images which are often also perceived just before falling asleep. Avoid preoccupation with these, and continue steady inner gazing. You may then see a mass of radiant light—gold, blue, or a combination of hues. Or there may be only a sensation of luminous light without form. Again, this light, like the initial sounds perceived, is due to the convergence of nerve forces in the brain centers.

Whatever you hear or see, know that behind the phenomena is the clear field of consciousness. It is this you want to experience. In the early stages of contemplative meditation, you may experience a mixture of perceptions, such as sound-light perception along with a degree of clear-awareness experience. Or you may move quickly past inner perceptions of sound or light and experience clear awareness almost immediately. However, knowing the stages of progression from possible initial perceptions to more clear states of awareness will enable you to shift attention from one level to another when necessary.

Clearly understand the meditation process. 1) Sit upright in a quiet place. 2) Breathe deeply two or three times to induce relaxation and centering, and to cleanse the lungs. Think of your relationship with God, with the all-pervading Life. 3) Direct your gaze to the spiritual eye and your attention to the higher brain centers. Let your awareness, in the early stages, also be in the spinal pathway, feeling that body forces are flowing back from the organs of sense to the spinal pathway and upward to the brain. 4) Contemplate the ideal of experiencing pure awareness. Introduce into the process the use of a mantra, if you feel inclined to do so. 5) Continue in a relaxed, attentive manner for the duration of meditation. 6) Enjoy the deep calm and silence. 7) Come out of meditation and maintain the inner awareness and calm.

Use the Procedures Which Produce Results for You

A multitude of meditation techniques are taught. Use the procedures which produce the best results for you. Use methods which have been proven to be effective, avoiding the temptation to innovate, until you are an advanced meditator. Remember, the process is simple, so do not complicate it.

If you want to use a Sanskrit mantra, use *hong-sa* synchronized with inbreathing and outbreathing, with attention flowing inward as prescribed. Continue until you experience clear awareness and you no longer need the technique.

During deep meditation and afterward, if you are centered and at peace with yourself, external sounds or environmental circumstances will not unsettle you.

Some meditators prefer sitting in a cross-legged posture. If you are comfortable, there is no reason you cannot meditate in this position. With rare exceptions, always meditate sitting up, because this posture is most conducive to maintaining an alert attitude. For persons who, for reasons of disability, cannot sit upright, a reclining position will have to suffice. You can also contemplate in a meditative mood before going to sleep and while in bed when you awaken during the night. But for positive results, meditate sitting upright when at all possible.

Learn to meditate alone, because this will enable you to give full attention to the process. Also, your private meditation practice will become a treasured routine which will anchor your life. You will experience success and become increasingly self-confident.

For shorter meditation sessions, meditating with family members who are also interested in the process can be enjoyable. This can be mutually reinforcing as well as helping to deepen relationships. Many people find that short meditations, practiced in a group, help greatly to contribute to harmony—in the family unit, in the work place, or wherever people are sharing common activities. Also, many find that coming together with friends and associates to meditate once a week is beneficial. Such group meditation sessions support individual resolve and benefit new persons who have only recently begun meditation practice; but for longer, in-depth meditation sessions it is best to meditate alone. There may be times when you will want to sit for a long time, experiencing inner states and contemplating your relationship with God and your place in the universe.

It is best, especially if you plan to meditate deep and long, not to eat heavily before meditation practice, because meditation slows body processes and this is not practical while food is being digested. Also, after eating, blood flows from the brain to the stomach, and mental alertness is sometimes impaired.

Things to Avoid While Meditating

Anticipate your meditation session and give yourself fully to the process which works for you. Leave your cares and worries outside of the meditation chamber. You will be better able to handle what needs to be handled after you meditate. Assure a quiet meditation environment, because you will want to give full attention to the inner process. Do not play mood music while meditating; do not listen to special recorded sounds or be involved with any outside influence. Avoid gimmicks and "modern innovations" which promise "quick results." The easy, natural way to meditate is already known and I have explained it here to you. Follow the guidelines. Surrender to the process. It is time-tested and works for every person who uses it correctly.

If you meditate when rested, in the proper posture and in the proper way, you will be able to avoid falling asleep while meditating. Some meditators report a tendency to drift into reverie or sleep when they begin to relax. This is a habit which can be overcome with practice. Some meditators with a prior history of being hypnotized also report such incidents. If enthusiasm is present, if desire to experience God-consciousness or pure awareness is present, and if meditation is practiced correctly, it will not be long before superconscious states prevail.

Avoid preoccupation with mental imagery while

meditating. This leads to fantasy and is contrary to the purpose of practice. Refrain also from being deluded into thinking that inner perceptions which seem to be informative are due to the influence of "spirit guides" or "inner guides." If you allow this, you are but playing with other aspects of your own mind and personality instead of becoming a mature Self-realized person. Any useful insights which surface in the mind have their origins in your own consciousness, or in the ocean of cosmic consciousness of which you are a part. Do not allow your consciousness to remain fragmented by believing in "other intelligences" which are supposed to influence you. Avoid involvement with persons who believe themselves to be able to "channel" information from beings residing in subtle spheres. This causes mental and emotional confusion and is based on faulty understanding.

Do not be proud of your presumed spiritual attainment and do not allow yourself to be driven by compulsions to share your "inner revelations" with the world. If you truly have something to share, you will know it, and circumstances will unfold to allow it. If you are compulsive about it, or driven by emotions, you should deepen your spiritual practices and prove your understanding in the arena of daily living.

Long-term Benefits of Meditation Practice

The benefits of meditation come from the complete relaxation experienced and the rest provided to the mind and body systems. When stress is minimal, internal forces can flow to perform their respective purposes, and superconscious influences can flow into the mental field, brain, nervous system, and body to nourish and renew. Regular meditation sessions of twenty to thirty minutes once or twice a day are effective in contributing to relaxation and a steady flow of superconscious influences. Merely by meditating on a regular schedule in order to obtain the obvious benefits, you will eventually experience increased spiritual awareness, improved function, and transformation of the mental field. Consciousness is processed through the mental field and physical body, so the more refined and responsive these are, the more free you will be to express in this world.

With spiritual unfoldment, there is certain to be improvement in psychological states. With spiritual and psychological health, physical wellness and environmental relationships will improve. As the individual becomes healthier in every way, so does society. Therefore, our spiritual practices are not for us alone, and our enlightenment also benefits all of humanity.

While engaged in meditation practice and all processes you know to be useful, do not think of yourself as a mere human being attempting to "become" a spiritual being. Know that you *are* a spiritual being, dutifully arranging conditions so that your shining nature can more fully be manifested.

Review

1. Meditation is the natural process of turning attention and internal forces back to their source.
2. Review the benefits of regular, correct meditation practice.

3. Review the process of meditation until you clearly understand it.

4. A mantra is a sound formula inwardly listened to which allows attention to flow to a chosen point of focus so that it does not remain involved with feelings and thought patterns.

5. Whatever you perceive, during meditation, if it is subject to change or modification, go beyond it to the experience of pure consciousness.

6. Anticipate your meditation session and give yourself fully to the process which works best for you.

7. Your inner intelligence already knows how to meditate. You need only practice correctly and then experience spontaneous unfoldment.

SELF-EVALUATION AND PLANNING

1. What meditation schedule have you decided upon?

2. Practice a short meditation session and observe the body's relaxation response and degrees of mental calm in relationship to diminished breathing.

3. After you have attained a degree of proficiency in meditation practice, invite a friend or two to meditate with you now and then.

4. After meditation, rest in the calm state for a while, then carry that inner calm into your activities and relationships.

5. Write a short paragraph which best describes your present aspiration for spiritual growth.

I have three treasures. Guard and keep them:
  The first is deep love,
  The second is frugality,
  And the third is not to dare to be ahead of
    the world.
Because of deep love, one is courageous.
Because of frugality, one is generous.
Because of not daring to be ahead of the
  world, one becomes the leader of the world.
                                   -Lao-tzu

It is easy in the world to live after the world's
  opinion; it is easy in solitude to live after
  one's own; but the great man is he who in
  the midst of the crowd keeps with perfect
  sweetness the independence of solitude.
                          -Ralph Waldo Emerson

The Lord is my light and my salvation; whom
  shall I fear? the Lord is the strength of my
  life; of whom shall I be afraid?
                               -Psalms 27:1

CHAPTER 5

Personal Responsibility: Path to Emotional Maturity

Our thesis is that each rational person is responsible for his or her wellness and spiritual growth, hence responsible for his or her inner happiness. Debate the matter if you will, complain, justify and rationalize as much as you want; the fact remains—we are responsible for our awareness of being and for all that proceeds from it.

While emotional maturity will occur gradually as we continue our spiritual practices and engage in routines which can contribute to reasonable success in various ventures, if we will attend to matters directly relating to emotional maturity, our growth will be more rapid and our successes more predictable. Many people fail to achieve their spiritual and material goals because

they refuse to "grow up," avoiding responsible behavior and defeating their own purposes. They have the
mistaken opinion that when they are enlightened,
when circumstances are perfect, or at least acceptable,
they will automatically be emotionally mature. This is a
grievous error in judgment, and only disappointment
can follow.

A first step in the direction of emotional maturity is
to confront the world as it is and accept certain things.
The laws of consciousness and mind are exact. Abide
by them and we prosper, refuse to abide by them and
we suffer. This is a fact of life. Another fact of life is that
there is pain to confront and handle; if not physical
pain, then trauma due to our having to come to terms
with circumstances beyond our control. We hurt when
we see someone injured in an accident. We hurt when
we see people we care about doing things which can
only result in misery. We grieve when someone special
to us moves away, or dies to the world. We look about
us and we see much misfortune, poverty, confusion, ex-
ploitation, selfish behavior, greed, and assaults against
nature. If we are very sensitive, we may even take issue
with nature's way of providing food for her creatures
by having them prey upon each other. For many people
life is hard, even miserable. There are always reasons
for what happens and there are always causes for effects, but we may not like the way nature functions.
Most of what occurs in nature will continue to occur
whether we approve of the processes or not; it is best,
therefore, for us to be responsible for what we can influence and to do our best to ensure our personal awakening and the awakening of others who are receptive to
learning.

In this world at least, we are human beings. A human being is a blending, a coming together, of spirit and matter. As spiritual beings, we are reflected lights of pure consciousness, using mind, brain, nervous system, and body. The mind is formed of very fine material and is electromagnetic in character. The body is formed of elements found throughout the realm of manifest nature. The body is of *humus*, of the soil, or material elements. The body has a beginning and it will have an end, at least in its present form. The elements, when released due to decomposition or cremation, will be used again and again to combine and form other aspects of nature. The spiritual nature, being permanent being, will continue to exist in subtle realms after departing from the body.

While coming to terms with circumstances in this world, come to terms with the fact that you will eventually leave this world, at transition. Ask yourself, "What do I want to accomplish during the years I have remaining in this present life cycle?" This can help you to get very honest with yourself, very self-responsible.

As life emerged on this planet, impulses interfered with fine matters to produce forms through which to express. The results of the impulses of evolution can be observed in simple life forms, plant and animal, through to higher animals and man. In man we have the highly developed brain structure which serves as a processing medium for mental activities. Lower life forms have rudimentary brains and nervous systems, and very simple life forms which lack brain and nervous system still register life impulses and reactions to the environment.

In common with many animals, man has a lower

brain, the area of the brain which is responsible for the body's survival, regulating as it does the many functions required to maintain body temperature, hormonal and chemical secretions, respiration, healing processes, and many more. We now know that some of these functions can be consciously controlled, through intention and trained use of mental imagery. Man also has the power of speech and the higher brain areas to allow for this. Man is a thinking being. Some animals may think, after a fashion, but they do not have well-developed language skills. Some even exhibit characteristics we say are human. We can see, at many levels of animal development, evidence of caring, affection, faithfulness, and willingness to learn.

Spirit-Mind-Body Interrelationships

Reasonably informed people have long known of the spirit-mind-body connection. Our degree of spiritual awareness influences mental processes as well as emotional states, and these in turn influence physical states. Some researchers today do not understand the spiritual nature of man, and so continue their investigations on the premise that man is a mind/brain-body entity only. Even so, many useful discoveries have been made, and are being made, but the fact remains that the full range of possibilities cannot be known unless man's spiritual nature is acknowledged and understood.

The spirit, through the mind/brain, is superior to body processes and to environmental circumstances. A spiritually aware person can, if willing, constructively alter body functions and even contribute to the regeneration of the body. Such a person can, through choice alone, decide to be free or to remain in bondage to circumstances. Addictions can be renounced and better habits adopted, easily and comfortably, by intention.

Studies at various medical research centers indicate the following: cancer patients who focus on imagery to relax experience an increase in levels of the hormone thymosin, which helps disease-fighting cells mature; when persons are confronted by loss, the hormone cortisone increases, and diminishes the number of disease-resisting T-cells in the blood; fear activates the adrenal glands, which produce cortisol and adrenalin, diminishing the body's immunity; helplessness causes certain white blood cells to become less effective; security bolsters the body's immune system; stress can result in production of cortisol by the adrenal glands, decreasing production of white blood cells and leaving the body more prone to infection. The combination of signals from nerves, hormones, and neuropeptides governs how susceptible a person will be to infection and various ailments, including cancer.

Emotions do play a role in body function, contributing to either wellness or a disease-prone condition. A spontaneous free flow of emotion is natural to a healthy person who is relating to his environment. What is harmful are sustained emotional states of a destructive nature.

Even when we are informed of the problems to which we may be contributing because of our unregulated emotional states, we often persist until damage is done before seeking help in the direction of a more responsible and mature way of living. All too often we ask for help only when we are ill. And, surprisingly, a fair percentage of those who seek professional help will not assume personal responsibility for their mental states, emotional states, and behavior, even when an educational program is offered. It is as though the willingness to die prevails.

What is it in human nature that so often causes a person to continue to do the very things which can only invite problems? It may be feelings of guilt, therefore the inner conviction that "I deserve to suffer." It may be willfulness, therefore an attitude of "I have a right to be me, and to be angry and resentful if I want to!" It may be loneliness, resulting in despair because "there is nothing to live for." It may be weakness, an unwillingness to be responsible and face up to a learning and growing process.

An increasing number of physicians are today working with patients who are willing to learn to be self-responsible, and dramatic healings are being reported. One doctor said, "Even among those who do not get well, many of them die happy."

For a person who believes that transition from the body is the end of life, hearing about patients who "die happy" may bring only momentary satisfaction. At least the patient did not overly suffer. However, those who understand that after transition the individual being continues to grow in understanding and to experience life in subtle realms, knowing of conscious, surrendered transition is cause for comfort—a blessing for the departed and an affirmation of the goodness of life for all currently embodied.

While it is true that chemicals and hormones influence emotions, emotional states also influence the body chemistry. The "placebo effect" is now well known because of widely published reports in various media. A placebo is an inert substance, incapable of causing any effect upon the body; yet often when a patient is given such a substance and told it is a helpful medicine, the brain will actually secrete substances into the blood which mimic opium and heroin, which then bind to pain receptors in the nervous system, blocking pain. These substances can also be released as a result of belief and the use of mental imagery techniques, without a placebo being prescribed or taken.

It is often possible to fairly accurately predict if a person will recover from a disease or if the disease will progress by reviewing the patient's psychological profile. Persons who are generally emotionally fulfilled and have a strong desire to be healthy and to continue their activities will most often get well. Persons who are not emotionally satisfied and who have very little to look forward to will often experience progressive deterioration and either become incapacitated or make their transition. Many will experience a reasonable degree of health and function but will manifest a continuing pattern of minor ailments and psychological problems.

As long as we live in the world of nature, we will have to be aware of influences from within and from without—those which originate from our states of consciousness and those which are environmental in origin. Therefore, our relationship with our world is important; this is why a responsible person will do everything possible to come to terms with it, cooperate with its rhythms, abide by its laws, and ensure the most ideal conditions for the maintenance and wellness of body and mind.

The universe is a play of cosmic forces. What we

receive from our environment can be beneficial or det-
rimental, depending upon what is received and how it
is received. The more spiritually aware we are, the
healthier we are, and the less we are influenced
adversely by environmental factors and the more we,
in turn, beneficially influence planetary consciousness.
Our total beingness—our states of consciousness, our
thoughts, and our feelings—radiates into the psychic,
mental, and material levels of nature, contributing in
ways small and large to the overall condition of the
planet. Because of this, we have a duty to be as
spiritually aware and as healthy as possible. We
contribute to social and planetary wellness to the degree that we are well. So now we must henceforth
consider spirit-mind/brain-body/planet interrelation-
ships.

We are often restricted from doing the things we
want to do because of self-defeating attitudes we habit-
ually maintain and nourish. Our thoughts, moods, and
behavior tend to reflect these destructive attitudes. A
responsible person will cheerfully enter into a program
of inner transformation by doing every practical thing
possible to contribute to useful change. Here are just a
few self-defeating attitudes we may find ourselves ver-
balizing from time to time, and alternative attitudes to
assume to replace them. If you have a degree of self-re-
spect, you will follow through and do what you have to
do to open yourself to desirable change. "A" is a sam-
ple self-defeating attitude; "B" is a constructive alternative. With practice you will find that you can adjust
your attitude at will, resulting in dramatic changes in
the way you think, feel, speak, perceive your world,
and behave.

A. "I feel so hopeless. I have so many problems and limitations."

B. "I am confident and purposeful. I will solve all problems and live a free and productive life. I rejoice in this opportunity!"

A. "I'm no good because I've made so many mistakes. I'm not worthy of anything better."

B. "I am a divine being, made in the image and likeness of God. The past is no longer an influence in my life. I am worthy of a satisfying, fulfilled life, and I am now doing my part to allow it to unfold in right order."

A. "I'm a failure. I always have been, and always will be."

B. "I see life as an adventure. I live as a mature and responsible person and enjoy experiencing growth and achievement."

A. "I never had a chance to be happy. No one motivated me."

B. "Happiness is grounded in my inner nature. I am self-motivated, inspired to constructive action, and enthusiastic about unfolding all possibilities."

A. "God doesn't exist. Even if He does, I can't know Him or experience His presence in my life."

B. "God is the single Life, Being, Power, and Substance. Because I am a ray of pure consciousness, I can know God and experience a conscious relationship with Him. I will do all I can to prepare myself to grow spiritually and live as I am meant to live."

A. "I'm unskilled; jobs are already taken and

money is scarce. There is nothing for me to do and no chance of making any real money."

B.   "I will acquire an education and find my true purpose in life. As I inwardly realize that 'I am in harmony with my world,' I am being led to the right circumstances where I can use my talents to the fullest. I live in an abundant universe which supplies all my needs."

A.   "I'm just naturally obese; it runs in my family."

B.   "My body is the temple of the Holy Spirit and is responsive to my attitudes and behavior. I maintain an inner mental picture of my ideal body weight and follow through in practical ways to bring this into manifestation."

A.   "I'm addicted (to alcohol, drugs, food, destructive behavior, etc.) and am a slave to my addictions."

B.   "I have freedom of choice and now decide to be so purposeful and goal-oriented that I am no longer attracted to substances or behavior which interfere with my purposes. I am free, self-determined, responsible, and constantly growing in the direction of total fulfillment."

A.   "No one loves me. I am so lonely."

B.   "I can never be lonely because I am on friendly terms with a friendly and supportive universe. I consciously acknowledge my inner divine nature, relate easily with others and enjoy friendships and satisfying personal relationships. I live, not out of need, but out of my increasing awareness of the goodness of life. I am happy!"

Sometimes by merely adjusting our mental attitudes we experience miracles in our lives. At other times, attitude adjustment is but the beginning, a good one, and we will have to follow through to learn to function better in order to experience desirable changes; but it all begins with a shift in consciousness and a change in the way we feel about ourselves and our relationships.

To be addicted is to be attached, either by conscious choice or because of emotional immaturity. Make no mistake about it, a person who is addicted has an immature personality. With responsible behavior comes maturity, and with maturity comes freedom from all attachments.

Usually we become attached to behavior because we have no real purpose. If we had real purpose, we would learn to solve problems, put away destructive and time-wasting behaviors, and move ahead in the direction of our worthy purposes. Without purpose we may feel inept, insecure, incapable of functioning. We may then turn to behavior which affords us a degree of satisfaction, or enables us to avoid thinking about our problems and challenges. The addictive person is not a happy person, and no degree of involvement in non-useful behavior is going to result in happiness. It may result, instead, in destructive relationships, neurosis, psychosis, and other forms of illness. An addictive personality is the screen between us and our potential good. Therefore, all addictions must be renounced if true happiness and personal fulfillment are to be realized.

An addictive personality is addicted to behavior, not to substances or relationships. Substances and relationships may be present, but the desired end of involvement with them is the feeling which results. One can even be addicted to thinking patterns, moods, and fantasy. Any form of dependency can be overcome with understanding and positive behavior. Positive behavior is almost always essential, because it is frequently almost impossible to think our way free of attachments. It can be done, however; and sensible behavior will follow.

The best way for most people to rid themselves of addictive behavior is to intentionally engage in a chosen program which will enable them to actually experience how it is to be different than they usually are, how to actually experience a balanced, integrated life.

The Beneficial Results of Positive Reinforcement

When I am talking with people, many of them tell me they feel almost overcome by circumstances—with job pressures, social obligations, effort to pay the bills, feelings of a need to conform to the expectations of others, and the many other things which press in upon them. They may say, "I don't feel in control of my life any more. I'm under so much pressure that I'm over-stressed and confused."

There is definitely something to be done to help us center ourselves. It is to consciously do something, every day, which is enjoyable and creative. It must be something we can do alone, although we may do it with others from time to time. It must be something we can engage in for at least one hour each day, either for a whole hour or in two 30-minute sessions. Such purposeful activity is positive reinforcement and enables us to be in charge of our lives for that duration of time in which we are involved with the project of our choice.

It may be brisk walking, swimming, or some other athletic activity, or it may be working in the yard or garden; but it must be something we enjoy doing and which will contribute to a sense of well-being. For some it will be an interlude of Hatha Yoga practice, for others it will be deep meditation.

During this period of positive reinforcement, nothing should be allowed to intrude or interfere. During this one hour you will be in control of your life. You will be doing something beneficial because you have chosen to do it. Your self-esteem will improve, your self-confidence will blossom, your powers of concentration will be enhanced, you will learn to be self-content because you engage in the chosen routine. If you allow circumstances to interfere, you are not in control of your life, and surely you deserve to be in control of your life for one hour a day!

As you adhere to your chosen program, you will notice that you are less stressed, more content, more agreeable with others, and more enthusiastic about life in general during occasions not directly related to your daily routine.

Remember, it must be something creative and enjoyable which you can do alone every day, making allowances for those rare occasions when a pressing circumstance might intervene. This practice reinforces your intention to live a purposeful life. It is proof that you are actually sincere about the matter and are willing to engage in useful procedures which can assist you to accomplish all of your other major goals.

Be Responsible for Your Behavior Under All Circumstances

You may behave appropriately in social circles, but how do you behave at home, with members of your family or when alone? Or perhaps you don't behave appropriately in public, because you don't know how or you don't care?

Are you courteous, supportive, well-mannered, and in all ways positive in your dealings with others? Or do you play personality games, compete, and display ignorance of the social graces?

Do you choose your friends and companions wisely, or do you associate instead with persons whose life styles are contrary to what you say you want yours to be? We are known to others by the companions we associate with on a routine basis. Are your relationships constructive and supportive? Do you bring out the best in your friends, and they in you? Or are you "hanging out" with the wrong people?

We should always discern the inner divine qualities of every person, while recognizing that personalities differ, and purposes differ. If you are intentionally over-socializing with people whose purposes differ from yours, whose life styles are not wholesome, whose behavior is destructive, you are asking for trouble. Maybe you do this because you want to fail? Maybe you do this because of low self-esteem? Maybe you do this because it has become a habit? Whatever the reason, if this has been your pattern, sincerely think about changing it. You should be so involved with constructive purposes that you have no time, or inclination, for such relationships.

It may be that you have grown and persons close to you have not. It also may be that to maintain a worthwhile relationship, while maintaining your personal integrity, can be a growth experience for you. Haven't you noticed how this can be, especially in family circles? Relationships are established and are, for the most part, worthwhile; but perhaps sometimes some things others do or say can challenge you. Learning to adapt and to be loving and supportive, without becoming upset or withdrawing, can be educational, as well as evidence of your degree of emotional maturity.

True love is the basis of all satisfying relationships, and not just on the human level. True love is total acceptance, and we will eventually mature to the point where we can honestly affirm that we totally accept all of nature, including all of its manifestations. When I refer to total acceptance, I am not equating love with attachment; I am saying that when we truly love, we are able to see everything in its proper place in the universe, and, if we want to, we can pronounce it "good."

Do you love truly? Do you accept totally the universe as it is? There are many things you may not like, or even approve of, as you view your world and think about it; but can you see through all surface appearances to the inner, divine core of nature? If you can— and you can with practice—you know how to truly love.

We do not have to approve of the behavior of people to love them. We can love the inner nature of others even when their outer character and behavior is discordant. In this way we can, if we are willing, gently encourage the emergence of ideal qualities in others, to assist them in the direction of growth and fulfillment.

Even if they are resistant, we can still love them, knowing that eventually righteousness will prevail.

A true love relationship is not a sexual one, although sexual attraction may be present. Not all who marry because of sexual attraction remain "in love" when the attraction fades. On the other hand, when love is present, husband and wife can experience a satisfying sexual relationship, even without the sometimes frantic emotionalism which may accompany intense sexual attraction.

Male and female are polar opposites, positive and negative. Man and woman are designed, by nature, to be attracted and to cooperate in fulfilling their purposes. Sometimes they mate for the enjoyment of it, and such intercourse can be intensely "spiritual." Sometimes they mate to have children, because they want them in the family unit or because they are fulfilling a natural urge to populate the planet by providing access to souls desiring experience here.

Sometimes, when personal expectations are not fulfilled, one may say, "I used to love that person, but now my love has turned to hate," as if love could ever be anything else but love. What they mean, of course, is that they thought they were in love, but when things didn't go their way, they became angry and spiteful.

It would be a more wonderful world if people always kept their agreements, but not all do. On the other hand, it would also be a more wonderful world if we didn't expect so much of others, on our own terms, and were more open to allowing life to meet our needs in ways only it knows best.

While doing our honest best to encourage supportive relationships with others, it is extremely helpful to look, not to individuals, but to the Source for our good. Support flows to us through others, but it does not originate with them.

We cannot live in this or in any world without relationships, if not with people, then with the forces of nature. It is essential, therefore, to learn to harmonize with nature on all levels, and this will be the theme for the following chapter. Study it carefully and apply everything you learn. Your willingness to do this, and to follow through, can make a remarkable difference in your life.

Review

1. You are responsible for your own wellness and inner growth, therefore, responsible for your own inner happiness.
2. We, as spiritual beings, are reflected lights of pure consciousness, using a mind, brain and nervous system, and body.
3. Emotions play a role in body function, contributing to wellness or a disease-prone condition. Be an emotionally mature person by accepting self-responsibility.
4. As long as we live in the world of nature, we will have to be aware of influences from within and without, those which originate from our states of consciousness and those which are environmental in origin.
5. The more spiritually aware we are, the healthier we are inclined to be, the less we are adversely influenced by environmental factors, and the

more we, in turn, beneficially influence society and planetary consciousness.

6. Banish all self-defeating attitudes and, if need be, joyously enter into a constructive transformation program.
7. Review the beneficial results of positive reinforcement.
8. Cultivate ideal qualities and unfold divine capacities.

SELF-EVALUATION AND PLANNING

1. Are you now a self-responsible person?

2. If not, what will you do to be more responsible?

3. List any self-defeating attitudes you have.

4. What attitudes will you cultivate to dissolve the destructive ones?

5. Are you aware of any addictions you have? What are they?

6. What will you do to banish them from your life?

The science of life is everlasting and bestows merit, prestige, happiness, longevity, livelihood and heaven.

-Sushruta Samhita

The person whose gastric fire is well-tended, who feeds it with wholesome diet, who is given to daily meditation, charity and the pursuit of spiritual salvation and who takes food and drinks that are agreeable to him, will not fall victim of approaching diseases except for special reasons. The disciplined person of even temperament lives for one-hundred years, blessed by good men and devoid of disease.

-Ayurvedic Axiom

For where there is love of man, there is also love of the art (of medicine). For some patients, though conscious that their condition is perilous, recover their health simply through their contentment with the goodness of the physician.

-Hippocrates

CHAPTER 6

Experience Total Wellness the Natural Way

Cooperation with the creative forces of nature is the way to complete spiritual understanding and mental, emotional, and physical wellness. It is the way to radiant living.

The principles of right living are known; they are easy to understand and require but personal discipline to adhere to them. Every person who is informed about how to live must assume self-responsibility for his or her own wellness. From time to time, if the assistance of a trained practitioner or physician is required to help us to be restored to balance, it is still up to the individual to participate totally if the healing process is to occur as speedily as it should. Nature heals and maintains balance—we can only open ourselves to nature's influences. An estimated eighty percent of the general ailments experienced by most people will be healed by the body's renewal powers, even without the aid of an outside agency. The ideal is not only to experience total wellness, but to ensure internal balance to the extent that discomfort and disease are not possible.

It is easier for us to satisfy our just desires and to fulfill worthy purposes when we are healthy and functional. But there is more—healthy long life also provides opportunity and time for the cultivation of higher values and for our spiritual practices, so that we fulfill soul destiny. While what now follows will be helpful to the average reader who may not yet be interested in spiritual values, I trust that the majority of readers will be inclined to embrace all aspects of life and to use this information to more fully enter into a balanced and conscious relationship with the forces of nature and the rhythms of the universe. I wish to serve everyone with useful guidelines and to assist purposeful readers in the direction of cosmic consciousness and forever freedom of spirit.

While much of what is included here is general knowledge, some is specialized knowledge which has long been known to a few and is now again being made available to a wider public. Many of the principles discussed may at first seem a bit difficult to understand. They really are not, but will require patient study and application before they are well-learned. The results of such learning will surely contribute much to your life, both in improved function and in a better comprehension of your place in nature's plan.

The specialized knowledge explained herein is the gift of Ayurveda, one of the oldest known systems of wellness on Earth. *Ayurveda* is a Sanskrit word made up of *ayus*, life, and *veda*, knowledge. Ayurveda is life knowledge. The system has roots in India and can be traced back at least five thousand years; References to it are to be found in the *Rig Veda*, the oldest body of reli-gious-philosophical literature known. The word *veda* means "to know." The Vedas are four in number, and while once believed to be a collection of poetry, history, and philosophy, they are today considered sources of insight into the nature of the world-as-consciousness for those who possess sufficient intellectual and intu-itive powers to discern the truth behind the words. The *Ayurveda* is a subordinate scripture in which the theme of health, medicine, longevity, and righteous living is emphasized. Included in the medicine category are the branches covering: ear, eyes, nose, throat, and mouth diseases; psychiatry; pediatrics; toxicology; and rejuve-nation and vitalization procedures. Extensive informa-tion on surgical procedures is also included.

Two of the better known Ayurvedic texts are the *Charaka Samhita* and *Sushruta Samhita*. The word *samhita* refers to wholeness or completeness. It is today be-lieved that knowledge of Ayurvedic procedures flowed along trade routes to Arabia, Greece, and Egypt, and later to all of Europe. It also spread through Tibet to Asia. It is a matter of historical record that Hippocrates, the Greek physician who lived during the fourth cen-tury B.C. and who was known as "the father of Western medicine," visited India, as did some Greek philoso-phers.

In recent years of this century several English translations of Ayurvedic texts have been published and have been made available in Europe and America. Ayurvedic medicine was the common mode of patient treatment in India until British influence resulted in the importation of what is known as Western medical prac-tice. Now, in India, the United States, and a few other countries, Ayurveda is again being recognized and its procedures more widely utilized. Clinics have been established, staffed by physicians trained in both Ayurvedic and Western medical procedures. It has recently come to my attention that in this country a national association of Ayurvedic Physicians has now been formed with over 800 medical doctors as members.

The Ayurvedic system is well researched, prevention-oriented, in most instances easily applied, free from harmful effects, economical, and aimed at treating the underlying causes of discomfort and disease rather than merely suppressing symptoms. In this approach the physician is more interested in knowing what kind of patient has the disease than in what kind of disease the patient has. The purpose is to find out the basic constitutional nature of the patient-client, then to prescribe what is needed to restore balance to mind and body. When internal systems are balanced and the immune system is strong, disease is unlikely. When inner peace is known and psychological harmony is established, even accidents are rare.

The Ayurvedic physician understands that the patient-client is really a spiritual being expressing through the mental field and physical body, and that if mental order and physical harmony are the norm, health will be natural and the person will more easily be responsive to cosmic forces flowing through nature. Health, then, is the natural condition of a person who is living in harmony with cosmic forces. Disease results from being in disharmony with these forces and in suffering and disequilibrium of principles and forces in mind and body. Furthermore, because nature's principles are universal, all living things can be examined and their internal condition understood. Four complimentary approaches are taken to assist a person in the direction of wellness:

1. *The Cultivation of Spiritual Awareness*—For complete benefits you should understand the importance of attending to all duties in life with the right attitude. You should understand the importance of spiritual practices, including regular meditation, in contributing to expanded states of consciousness. You will then be more inclined to live a natural and spontaneous life and will tend to think, feel, and behave in harmony with the order of the universe. As a result stress will be minimal in the body, and internal balance more likely. Radiant health will be experienced and disease will be absent, because no underlying causes for it can exist.

2. *The Ordering of Personal Environment*—Recognizing that we all react to environmental circumstances, your personal environment should be as orderly and stress-free as possible so as not to contribute to disorganization of mental states, emotional unrest, or physical discomfort. Your environment includes everything with which you relate. Further, you will be encouraged to actively work to create an ideal social environment for others and in this way contribute to social wellness and planetary harmony.

3. *Behavior Modification*—Guidelines are given for diet, personal hygiene, exercise, and other life-enhancing procedures, as well as daily and seasonal routines which contribute to the restoration of inner balance and to harmonizing of biological rhythms. Many healthy people naturally adhere to many of these guidelines. Through behavior modification, proper nutrition, and

other means we learn to adapt to cosmic influences and resist environmental challenges which might be encountered from time to time.

4. *Specific Therapeutic Regimens*—These include cleansing procedures, special dietary recommendations when needed, and whatever else may be necessary to restore the patient-client to psychological and physical health. Prescribed may be counseling, the use of herbal substances, and the administering of rejuvenation procedures. In short, whatever is needed to restore balance to the systems can be used.

An Ayurvedic physician begins by carefully and completely diagnosing the patient-client's total condition in order to arrive at an understanding of the basic constitution and symptoms. Included is a thorough questioning of the patient-client in order to hear his point of view and obtain background information, as well as to make a psychological evaluation. Then follows physical examination, with emphasis upon discerning evidence of subtle causes of complaints. Pulse diagnosis, refined to a high degree, is an important procedure. No symptom, not even vague complaint, is ignored. Everything the physician learns and observes is considered to be important. Mild neurotic tendencies may, for instance, contribute to internal imbalance leading later to more serious physical problems.

The Governing Principles Which Regulate Internal Processes

In the Ayurvedic approach to total wellness, the influences of certain *governing principles* are essential to the understanding of why various therapeutic strategies are considered. If you have carefully studied the earlier sections of this book, you will now more easily comprehend the following explanations about the governing principles of nature. The three major governing principle influences are *Water, Fire,* and *Air.* These are referred to, respectively, as *Kapha, Pitta,* and *Vata.* These principles are not actually the elements themselves, but the *influences* of the material causes of them. To explain further: The water governing principle is a combination of water and earth, with water predominating. Fire is a combination of fire and water, with fire predominating. Air is a combination of air and space, with air predominating. Remember this when Water, Fire, and Air governing principle influences are referred to hereafter. Also, all of the element influences are present in some degree in any one element influence or governing principle, with the named influence being the major one.

These governing principles are present in all the forms of nature, including the foods we eat. Because of this, anything in nature can be prescribed as a therapeutic agent if its specific qualities are known and if it is administered correctly.

In this system each person is born with a basic constitution, a basic characteristic psychosomatic nature resulting from element influences contributed by one's parents and modified by environmental circumstances. This is why we are different, as embodied beings. The ideal would be to have all three governing principles—Water, Fire and Air—in balance, but this is almost never the case. However, to contribute to the development of this ideal state of balance you can meditate, cultivate constructive thinking habits, remain calm and emotionally balanced, adjust personal behavior, attend to specific dietary plans, and do anything else which is useful to this purpose.

When one or more governing principles are aggravated, or increased in influence to a point where major disharmony and imbalance prevail, you may be inclined to experience changes in mood, behavior, or physical function. Likewise, if certain governing principles are suppressed, disharmony will also result. It is within range of available therapeutic strategies to bring about harmony among the three governing principles which prevail in mind and body.

The following information will be of help in understanding the influences of the three governing principles:

1. *Water-Element Influences*—Bodily stability, energy, lubrication, unctuousness (oily-greasy). Psychological effects are attachments, tendency to accumulate, and willingness to forgive others. This governing principle is aggravated by lack of physical exercise, sedentary habits, eating of too many sweets, acidic, salty, and oily foods, or too much milk, sugar, fat, and sweet fruits. Heaviness, drowsiness, itching of skin, and constipation can result.

2. *Fire-Element Influences*—Body heat, internal body temperature, digestion, power of perception (eyesight). The psychological effects are understanding, intelligence, anger, hate, jealousy. This governing principle is aggravated by fear, anger, grief, too much physical exercise, incomplete digestion, and eating too many foods which are bitter, acidic, salty, and dry. Hyperacidity, fainting, perspiration, excessive thirst, paleness of skin, and delirium can result.

3. *Air-Element Influences*—Movement, breathing,

natural urges to eliminate waste products, tissue trans-formation, sensory functions. This governing principle is aggravated by excesses of any kind, grief, anxiety, fear, strain or stress of any kind, suppression of natural urges, and hard falls or serious accidents. Stiffness, rough skin, shivering, hoarseness of voice, yawning, dryness, thirst, and sad moods can result. A sense of fear and emptiness and general anxiety may be charac-teristics of a person in whom the Air governing princi-ple is very strong.

Since the governing principles pervade all of na-ture, including the body, when they are in balance per-fect health and function are automatically experienced. When they are not in harmony, disorder tends to fol-low. Air governing principle influences the movements of prana—life force—in the body, and disturbances of the Air governing principle can upset the equilibrium of energy flows. The practice of certain breathing exer-cises can assist in maintaining the balance of the Air governing principle.

Psychological conditions can change the balance of the governing principles of the body. Strong emotions, positive or negative, contribute to either health and function or disease and premature death. Rigid beliefs and emotional states can contribute to actual changes in body chemistry, which changes can be beneficial or det-rimental, depending upon their character. The inten-tional cultivation of optimism, faith, and happiness strengthens the immune system and causes all body functions to improve. Habits of pessimism, fear, grief, depression, and a feeling of alienation from life can weaken the immune system and impair body function.

When symptoms are recognizable, they are evi-

dence of deeper causes which have been present at subtle levels for a much longer period of time. The purpose
of Ayurvedic therapies is not only to eliminate symptoms, but also to remove the underlying subtle causes
so that the problems will not arise again. When a person is self-responsible for his own wellness, he will be
able to maintain a lifestyle which will encourage permanent wellness. The Ayurvedic physician prescribes
and gives emotional support, but the patient-client is
the one responsible for final results.

Except for harmful influences introduced into the
body, diseases arise from within as the result of internal
disturbance. The body's immune system is quite capable of resisting the intrusion of viruses and other poten-
tially threatening agents if the person is healthy and the
governing principles are in balance. In fact, one of the
key purposes of Ayurvedic regimens is to ensure a
strong immune system and to encourage the internal
"fires" which are capable of metabolizing foods and
transforming them into needed substances. When the
internal fire is weak, the process of digestion, metabolism, and nutrient transformation is impaired. Toxins
accumulate which clog the systems and interfere with
function, weakening the various body systems. Purification procedures may be prescribed to remove toxic
matter so that health can be restored. Daily elimination
of normal waste products is encouraged as routine. The
three major waste products are feces, urine, and perspiration. These products are not totally waste; they are in
fact essential to the function of the food transformation
cycle.

For instance, feces supply nutrients through intestinal tissues before being eliminated as waste. They

also maintain strength and tone in the large intestine. The urinary system removes salt, water, and urea (nitrogenous waste) from the body. Urine is produced in the large intestine and helps to maintain the balance of water electrolytes (electrical conductors) within the body fluids. Normal urine production is essential to maintaining normal blood pressure and volume. If urine production is scanty, it may be because water is being retained in the tissues of the body. Perspiration helps maintain body temperature, carries off wastes, keeps the skin pores healthy, and it benefits the skin by promoting smoothness and elasticity. Perspiration, if massaged into the skin and allowed to dry before bathing, cleanses and softens the skin.

The Seven Tissues of the Physical Body

Seven tissues, the results of food transformation, comprise the "constructing elements" of the body. They maintain the functions of the different organ systems and vital parts, and they are also part of the protective mechanisms of the body. All of them are the result of inner fire, the transforming influence, fulfilling its purposes. In sequence these tissues are:

1. *Plasma*-Contains nutrients; transports them throughout the body to build and maintain organs and systems. In women, contributes to the formation of breast milk and menstrual fluid.

2. *Blood*-Carries nutrients and oxygen (also life force from oxygen) and transports carbon dioxide from the inner parts of the body to the lungs, there to be exhaled.

3. *Muscle*-Covers some organs and provides movement to joints so that functions can be performed.

4. *Fat*-Maintains lubrication and provides insulation against a cold environment.

5. *Bone*-Supports the body structure.

6. *Marrow*-Soft, fat vascular tissue inside the bones. Nerve tissue is of a similar tissue characteristic and carries motor and sensory impulses.

7. *Reproductive Tissue*-The end result of nutrient transformation; it makes possible reproduction of the species.

If preliminary supporting tissues are deficient, the *ones following will suffer.* For radiant health, it is important that the transformative fires be strong and that all governing principles remain balanced. The final result after the seven successive stages have been completed is *life essence* itself. This fine essence imparts radiance to the body, brilliance to the mind, and magnetism to the personality. An inner light emanates into the environment and shines for others to see. It is also accumulated in the body as a result of meditation, calmness, pure thinking, and purposeful living. It is wasted through excessive talk, restlessness, stress, dissipation of any kind, and poor health habits.

The Universe is Within Us as Well as Around Us

What occurs in the cosmos occurs in the body of man— the universe is within us as well as around us. There is really no retaining surface, in body or mind, where we leave off and the larger world begins. Our bodies are formed of the same substance of which the cosmos is formed, and the same governing principles and forces flow through everything. This is why perfect internal balance is only possible when we are in harmony with all of the forces and expressions of nature. By understanding our own internal processes we can more easily understand the processes of our larger, cosmic body.

Determining Your Basic Psychosomatic Constitution

Every person is born with a basic psychosomatic constitution, which remains generally the same throughout his life. The Greek word *psyche* means soul, but it is often defined as spirit, soul, or mind, with mind being the commonly accepted definition. *Somatic* refers to the physical body. Because of variables, no two people are identical as far as their psychosomatic constitutions are concerned. In relation to the three governing principles, a person may possess one of several possible governing principle constitutions, depending upon the dominant influences and the possible combinations. A person may be predominantly Water, Fire, or Air; or Water-Fire, Water-Air, Fire-Water, Fire-Air, Air-Water, Air-Fire, or Water-Fire-Air. These ten constitutional types will vary according to the percentage of mixtures of governing influences. Governing principle influences are determined at conception due to the combined characteristics of the parents, their environmental circumstances, time and circumstances of intercourse, circumstances surrounding the mother during the gestation period, the mother's spiritual and psychological state, and the food she eats. We see, then, how intricate the process of determining individual constitutional types can be. We cannot do anything about what we were provided with at birth as far as our basic psychosomatic constitution is concerned, but we can do something about the matter once we are sufficiently informed and determined to make changes in the direction of balance.

The Influences of the Three Qualities of Nature

The three qualities of nature—elevating, activating, and heaviness—are present throughout the universe, on all levels. They influence mind and body. The degree of individual spiritual awareness is also influential; one's constitutional nature is not static but because of various internal and external forces, it is constantly being modified. The elevating influence in nature tends to contribute to order of mind and body, and to influence function in the direction of harmony. The activating influence tends to contribute to motion and change. Heaviness contributes to inertia and non-change. The cultivation of elevating tendencies, then, is useful to higher purposes.

Because of the intimate interrelationship of mind and body, the body being considered an extension of the mind, what occurs in the mind influences body function and what occurs in the body tends to influence mental states. It therefore follows that the cultivation of constructive mental states is useful if someone desires to express through a healthy and functional body. Superior soul awareness virtually assures a healthy mental condition which, in turn, reflects in body function. A person who is spiritually aware is naturally inclined to always think correctly and to do spontaneously those things which will ensure health of body and harmony with the environment. The degree of ability to comprehend and outlook on life are strongly influenced by these three qualities of nature.

That we can, by commitment and discipline, be intentionally involved with our spiritual unfoldment and overall wellness is clear. Heaviness and darkness can be dissolved from the mind as the result of wise behavior, and restlessness can be neutralized as the result of cultivating the moral qualities and experiencing spiritual growth.

A Simple Self-Examination for Determining the Basic Constitution

When taking this examination, consider the characteristics in relationship to your life cycle from earliest memory to the present time, because certain presently existing characteristics may be due to minor changes recently experienced. Do not think of any characteristic as good or bad, but simply respond as honestly as you can. Unless you are using this text as your personal workbook, you may want to write the answers on a separate sheet of paper.

Once you have determined your basic psychosomatic constitution, everything else you read in this chapter will be more meaningful to you, because you will be able to relate the information given to your own situation.

If two or three answers seem to you to be almost equally true, select the one which is most accurate. Bear in mind that for a thorough determination you may

Characteristic	Water	Fire	Air
1. Body	( ) Broad shoulders, hips	( ) Moderate	( ) Narrow shoulders, hips
2. Weight	( ) Heavy	( ) Medium	( ) Thin (tendons show)
3. Endurance; strength	( ) Good	( ) Fair	( ) Poor
4. Skin	( ) Oily, pale, moist, white	( ) Soft, fair, oily, delicate pink to red	( ) Dry, rough, cool, darker
5. Skin aging	( ) Smooth, few wrinkles	( ) Freckles, moles, pigmentation	( ) Dry, flaky, wrinkles
6. Hair	( ) Oily	( ) Medium	( ) Dry
7. Hair Color	( ) Medium blonde, medium to dark brown	( ) Light blonde, red, light brown	( ) Dark brown to black
8. Hair texture	( ) Straight or wavy, thick	( ) Wavy, fine, soft	( ) Curly, kinky
9. Digestion, appetite	( ) Moderate, no extreme hunger	( ) Sharp hunger	( ) Irregular or heavy diet, but stays thin
10. Teeth	( ) White, large, little decay	( ) Yellowish, moderate size	( ) Large, protruding, crooked
11. Eyes	( ) Large, blue or brown	( ) Hazel, green, gray	( ) Small, black or brown
12. Elimination	( ) Heavy, slow, thick	( ) Soft, oily, loose	( ) Dry, hard, tendency to constipation
13. Sex drive	( ) Cyclical, infrequent	( ) Moderate	( ) Frequent
14. Physical activity	( ) Calm, steady	( ) Aggressive, intelligent	( ) Flighty, restless

114

	Water	Fire	Air
16. Voice, speech	( ) Low-pitched, melodious, slow, monotone	( ) Medium-pitched, sharp, laughing	( ) High-pitched, fast, dissonant, vibrato, weeping
17. Taste, food preferences	( ) Dry, light, low-fat, sweet, pungent	( ) Medium, light, sweet, warm, bitter, astrigent	( ) Oily, heavy, sweet, soupy, salty, sour
18. Sleep pattern	( ) Deep, prolonged, easy	( ) Sound, medium	( ) Short, insomnia
19. Memory	( ) Long-term memory	( ) Good, not prolonged	( ) Short-term memory
20. Financial behavior	( ) Saves regularly	( ) Saves, but spends on luxuries	( ) Money quickly spent
21. Reaction to stress	( ) Indifferent, complacent, withdraws	( ) Angry, jealous, irritable	( ) Fearful, anxious
22. Dreams	( ) Water, ocean, river, lake, erotic	( ) Fire, war, violence, strife, anger	( ) Fearful, flying, running, jumping
23. Mental predisposition	( ) Stable, logical	( ) Judging, artistic	( ) Questions, theorizes
24. Resting radial pulse (quality)	( ) Slow, moves like a swan	( ) Moderate, jumps like a frog	( ) Thready, slithers like a snake
25. Radial resting pulse (number of beats per minute)	( ) 60–70	( ) 70–80	( ) 80–100 plus
	Subtotal Water _____ times 4= _____	Subtotal Fire _____ times 4= _____	Subtotal Air _____ times 4= _____

Approximate body type, based on highest subtotal: _____

want to be examined by a qualified therapist, who may be able to discern things about you that you cannot see for yourself. This is but a general self-test and will provide basic information useful to you in your attempt to better understand yourself.

Ways in Which Governing Principles are Modified

Governing principles are balanced in the system by our state of consciousness, the thoughts we think, the emotions we express, the foods we eat, and the environment. They are forces which are subject to modification, so we need not think in terms of our present constitutional nature being fixed or unchangeable; it can be somewhat altered in favor of a more harmonious condition, if such modification is required, by our own efforts in the right direction.

If, for any reason, the governing principles of Water, Fire, or Air are upset, the symptoms of problems associated with each principle can be observed. These symptoms can be mild, medium, or pronounced. If the imbalance is mild, only a little discomfort may be experienced; if medium, more discomfort would be experienced; and if the imbalance is pronounced, serious discomfort or a diseased condition would be obvious. The governing principles are subtle influences, but their effects are manifested in the mind and body.

An undue increase or aggravation of the Air governing principle (the movement and circulating principle) may be evidenced by harshness of speech, emaciation, swarthiness of skin, throbbing of the limbs, desire for hot foods, insomnia, lack of vitality, constipation,

tremors, impairment of the functions of the sense organs, giddiness, depression, roughness of the skin,
sometimes loss of consciousness, atrophy of bone marrow, fear, anxiety, and grief. With decrease of the Air
governing principle the symptoms are diminished
movement, depression, and weakness of limbs; the patient-client is also predisposed to diseases due to increase of the Water governing principle, such as anorexia, nausea, and variability of appetite.

When the Fire governing principle is increased, it
may cause desire for cold foods and liquids, decreased
sleep, loss of strength, weakness of the senses, fainting,
yellow coloration of feces, urine, and skin, excessive
hunger or thirst, burning sensations, hyperacidity,
weakening of vital essences in the body, and a bitter
taste in the mouth. When this governing principle is decreased, the symptoms may be sour stomach, anorexia,
indigestion, tremors, heaviness, pallor of nails and
eyes, increase of mucus, lack of body luster, stiffness,
and irregular burning and pain sensations.

When the Water governing principle is increased,
symptoms may include coldness, heaviness, depression, fixed sensation in joints, dullness of appetite,
cough, light-colored stools, a feeling of fullness of body,
blocking of channels through which fluids and subtle
body forces flow, fainting, whiteness of skin, and sleep-
iness. When this governing principle is decreased,
symptoms may be dryness, absence of watery substances in usual places of the body except in the stomach, thirst, giddiness, general debility, looseness of
joints, wakefulness, tachycardia, dehydration, aching,
burning, heat, trembling, and loss of consciousness.

Unless overly influenced by dietary and other factors, the governing principles are usually influenced during different seasons, according to the preponderance of the governing influence active during each season. Because seasonal changes may occur differently in different parts of the world, adaptation would have to be made when ascertaining them and their present influences.

Usually, with an increase of any governing principle in the body, a person feels inclined to avoid anything that might cause further increase, and instead is led to do those things which would reduce the influence and increase the influence of the governing principles which are at the time naturally decreased in the body. Therapeutic regimens prescribed to balance the governing principles would include any useful approach to meet the needs. These might include internal cleansing, massage (dry or with oils), rest or activity, psychological counseling, meditation, dietary routine, and the use of herbs.

Herbal remedies sometimes prescribed are nontoxic and result in side benefits without complicating side effects.

Flowing With the Rhythms of the Universe

When we live in harmony with nature, our internal rhythms flow in accord with the rhythms of the universe. Since many people in the modern world do not always live in harmony with nature, it is well that we learn a little about how to do so. The body has marvelous powers of adaptation, but we should do the best we can to cooperate with nature's trends.

All of nature, including man, is influenced by the

seasons, due to the movement of Planet Earth around the sun. Nature is also influenced by the hours of sunlight and darkness, the gravitational pull of the moon and sun, and the sun's reflected light from the moon. During autumn, the Air governing principle is influential in nature, and Air-related problems can occur in people in whom the Air governing principle is naturally pronounced. In winter, the Water governing principle is influential in nature, and Water-related problems can occur in people in whom the Water governing principle is pronounced, causing colds, respiratory difficulties, and the like. During spring, the Water governing principle gives way to Fire, and the accumulated Water conditions are reduced. During summer, the Fire governing principle is influential in nature, and Fire-related problems can occur in people in whom the Fire governing principle is pronounced.

You should therefore do those things which would reduce the governing principles in your body which correspond to the seasons. In this way health and function can more easily be maintained. During autumn, you would begin to change over from a summer dietary program to one more suitable for the winter months, making gradual changes as the new season approaches and progresses. During winter, you would eat foods which result in increase of Fire and Air governing influences; and during spring, you would begin to change from a winter diet to one which is more suitable for summer, making the changes gradually as summer approaches. During winter, for instance, your diet could include foods that are heavier and heat-producing, while during summer, the diet could include foods which are lighter and cooling, with more liquids and more fresh fruits and vegetables. You would also dress appropriately for the different seasons—warmer during the colder months and lighter clothing during the warm seasons. Most of the obvious things come naturally to us, but our food choices do not always come so naturally, because of a tendency to eat what appeals to the senses but not necessarily what provides the body with its needs.

During the day, the governing principles are influential at regular intervals. From 6:00 to 10:00 A.M., the Water governing principle is predominant. At this time your body is made ready for the day's activities, and internal secretions, including the glandular secretions, are in motion due to the Air influence just prior to dawn. You may feel a little heavy, but with energy emerging. This is also your body's cleansing cycle, when waste products are eliminated, so it is the ideal time to attend to bathroom routines. Persons with predominantly Water constitutions may not want to eat breakfast, because this can increase the Water governing principle of the body.

From 10:00 A.M. until 2:00 P.M., the Fire governing principle is strongest, and this is the ideal time to schedule the major meal of the day. Digestive fire is strong at this time. A short rest after the midday meal would be in order, if convenient.

From 2:00 to 6:00 P.M., the Air governing principle is influential, and you may feel lighter but beginning to tire from the day's activities. The early evening hours are a good time to relax and meditate, then have a light meal. A short walk would be useful after the evening meal. From 6:00 P.M. until 10:00 P.M., the Water governing principle is again influential, and there is a natural inclination to eliminate body waste and prepare for sleep.

From 10:00 P.M. to 2:00 A.M., the Fire governing principle is again dominant, and the Air governing principle once more becomes influential until 6:00 A.M.

These internal changes occur naturally and are in harmony with the rhythms of nature. Arranging your life so that activities are scheduled in harmony with the natural environmental rhythms is very useful in contributing to health and function.

A Practical Way to Start the Day

The first thing upon awakening in the morning, breathe a prayer of thanksgiving and look forward to the day presently unfolding. If you have planned the day's activities the night before, you will be better able to begin with enthusiasm.

1. *Eliminate Body Wastes*-Evacuate your bowels and bladder and bathe your body, cleaning all body openings to remove accumulated waste matter. Rinse your mouth with clean water, massage the gums, and brush your teeth.

2. *Light Stretching Exercises*-This would be a good time to engage in gentle stretching exercises to encourage blood circulation and to awaken forces in your body. Many people like to use this time for a short session of Hatha Yoga practice.

3. *Practice Meditation*-Sit quietly and meditate, following your usual routine. Experience the deep silence and feel yourself to be in harmony with the universe. After meditation, pray for others and for the world and then begin your day.

It is a good plan to retire earlier at night to allow time for these important morning routines.

Persons with predominantly Air and Fire constitutions may want to eat a light breakfast, although this is a matter of preference. Your own feeling about the matter is the best guide.

Exercise Programs for the Basic Constitutions

Individuals with predominantly Water governing principle constitutions, because of their tendency to be complacent, often avoid regular exercise. They are the very ones who should engage in and thrive on a program of regular and sustained exercise.

Those with Fire governing principle constitutions may not have as much stamina, although they usually enjoy exercise. They should not overdo it, however, because their basic nature may cause them to be too competitive.

Persons with Air governing principle constitutions may be too frantic in their exercise programs, because of their already restless and active natures. Frantic exercise would only aggravate the Air principle, causing them to be hyperactive and to overly tire themselves.

A good general rule is to avoid extremes, while ensuring regular exercise in a manner which best suits the basic constitution. Especially with running, cycling, action sports such as tennis, or other competitive sports, the pace should not be exhausting. A more useful approach is to exercise to the point of feeling comfortably exhilarated, with a sense of well-being and serene joy. Swimming, walking, hiking in the woods or low mountains, and any exercise performed at a comfortable pace is ideal. Extremes should be avoided, because they overwork the body systems and interfere with the inner calm generated by meditation and cultivation of the inner life.

Several times a week, exercise should be engaged in which is sufficiently vigorous to stimulate the cardio-vascular system and force deeper breathing. This will maintain strength of the body, provide extra oxygen, and cleanse the tissues of carbon dioxide and other accumulated waste products. After a cooling-down period a bath can be taken, followed by a short rest period.

Of special value is a regular routine of Hatha Yoga practice. While this does not come under the heading of vigorous exercise, the practice of the various routines will strengthen muscles, impart flexibility, improve glandular function, and stimulate blood circulation. Subtle life forces will also be beneficially influenced, and dormant forces will be awakened. Hatha Yoga should be experienced in a meditative mood during which one is relaxed and attuned to inner processes. In this way, spiritual awareness is encouraged and you are more easily attuned to cosmic forces.

Experience the Healing Forces of Nature

Now and then, walk barefoot on the grass. This will energize the body and help to balance out its forces. Spend time by an ocean or a lake. Walk in the mountains. Experience the solitude of the desert. Swim when you can in an open body of water or in a swimming pool if a lake or ocean is not convenient. Feel yourself to be one with nature.

Daily, spend time out of doors to experience the normalizing effects of full-spectrum light. Do not wear your glasses during this time; allow the light to flow through the eyes to nourish the glands and systems of the body. Artificial light, without the full range of the spectrum in it, can contribute to chemical changes in the body, and even disease. Even indoors, people become more cheerful and productive when full-spectrum light sources are present, instead of light bulbs and tubes, which are deficient in some of the colors of the spectrum. If you must use sunglasses from time to time, use only grey-tinted lenses, not colored ones. The latter will prevent the complete range of color from entering through the eyes and optic nerves, and from these to the brain and pituitary gland.

Listen to the wind, soar with the clouds, commune with living things, and appreciate animals and all forms of life. You will increasingly find the universe to be your friend, benevolent and supportive. You will have no enemies and your timing will always be synchronized.

Food as Nourishment and Consciousness

Just as everything in the universe is a manifestation of the One Life, so food is consciousness. The food we eat not only provides the carbohydrates, proteins, vitamins, minerals, enzymes, and other necessary nutrients; it also provides life force, the influences of the three attributes in nature, and the three governing principle influences which determine internal states.

Food selection and preparation, then, should be a conscious exercise because the end results will affect body, mind, and spiritual awareness.

How we acquire our food is important. If harvested, it should be collected with care and thankfulness. If purchased or received from another by whatever means, it should be obtained honestly and in a spirit of appreciation. Food which is dishonestly acquired or paid for with resources which have been dishonestly accumulated will not have as wholesome an effect upon mind or body. An attitude or feeling of dishonesty will taint the mind and emotional nature, resulting in less than ideal effects from the eating of such food.

Fresh, live food sources should be selected for personal use and for serving to family members or guests. Persons employed in a food service business, such as a produce store or restaurant, should be aware that they are offering food as consciousness to buyers and customers. In this way any transaction becomes a spiritual exercise which benefits both seller and buyer.

Food should be prepared in a clean, quiet environment. Everything involved in the process, from the state of consciousness of the person preparing the food to the utensils used in preparation, should be sattvic, pure, and elevating. Always wash your hands well before beginning food preparation. A sick person, or one who is angry, moody, or emotionally disturbed, should not prepare food for others.

By using the following approach, even though foods are often recommended to meet the special needs of the different constitutional types, you will have a wide variety of ingredients available to satisfy basic nutritional requirements. A balance of carbohydrates, proteins, vitamins, and other nutrients will be naturally available in suitable quantities if a sensible dietary plan is used. The major emphasis is ensuring that the governing principles—Water, Fire, and Air influences—are properly considered to meet individual needs.

The approach to this matter is unique to this system in that it deals with the *tastes* of foods, because it is the taste which influences the governing principles in the body. You may find this a bit strange, but you will understand it better when we examine the origins of the various tastes.

Six tastes are recommended at most meals, except in special instances when tastes are provided in greater measure for specific purposes. The combination of Earth and Water elements in nature produces the sweet taste; the combination of Earth and Fire produces the sour taste; the combination of Water and Fire produces the salty taste; the combination of Air and Space (Ether) produces the bitter taste; The combination of Earth and Air produces the astringent taste; and the combination of Fire and Air produces the pungent taste.

It is easy to see that foods containing the governing principles which correspond to the governing principles influencing the body will have their effects. For instance, sweet, sour, and salty tastes will increase the Water governing principle and decrease Air. Pungent, bitter, and astringent tastes will increase Air and decrease Water. Pungent and salty tastes will increase Fire. Sweet, bitter, and astringent tastes will decrease Fire. Simply put, if the governing principle is present in foods according to their tastes, these principles will increase corresponding influences in the body. If they are absent, that influence in the body will be decreased. This is an easy way of selecting foods to contribute to the balancing of the governing principles of the body, and such body influences will also affect mental and emotional states.

Water should not be taken in large quantities for

about one hour before or after a meal, because it tends to dilute the digestive juices. Water taken before a meal may cause weight loss, and water after a meal may cause weight gain. Milk and soups can be taken with the meal in moderate quantities. Honey, if used as a sweetener, should not be used in excess and always in a natural state, not heated, because heating destroys the nutrient value.

The amount of food eaten at any one meal should be moderate. The general advice is to fill the stomach only about one-third full, perhaps the amount of food which would fill the cupped hands, but this is merely a statement to give a general idea. The better way is to eat in a relaxed mood, chewing your food well to assist digestion, and eating only until you feel comfortable and still maintain a feeling of lightness.

By following this well-balanced dietary plan, you will have no difficulty providing the body with all essential nutrients. If special needs arise, they can be easily met, and a qualified specialist may at times be helpful. It is always a good idea to avoid extremes, since such behavior is inconsistent with a natural and spontaneous lifestyle.

A common mistake made by persons new to a vegetarian food plan is to attempt to replace meat by eating too many dairy products, especially cheese and eggs, or to consume too many nuts or other vegetable protein sources. With common sense and by following natural inclinations, you will have no difficulty providing adequate protein for the body. I recommend a vegetarian diet, although this may not be suitable for everyone.

Herbs can be used for seasoning foods and for their

therapeutic effects, but salt and refined sugars should be eliminated entirely from the kitchen and the dining area.

When we eat foods, we are interacting with the cosmos. We interact with the cosmos through all of our senses, but it is with the food that we take into the body, in material form, that forces enter which are directly influential. The atomic structures of carbohydrates, proteins, vitamins, and minerals are not very different, varying only in combination, not in their essence. Below the level of the atom are finer forces which have their origins in the field of pure consciousness. Nature has provided us with everything necessary for function and completion of purposes, and an all-pervading intelligence directs every process of nature. When, through intelligent behavior, we learn to cooperate with nature's laws, we are able to consciously enter into a useful working relationship with the cosmos. The selection and eating of food, then, while requiring only a small portion of our time and attention, is a conscious practice which can be useful to our ultimate ends.

The most practical way to select foods is to follow your natural instinct and eat what your body "tells you" it wants. When the body is cleansed of toxic wastes, when one's lifestyle is ordered, when inner peace is present, we naturally feel inclined to select foods which are most useful for physical and emotional wellness. At such time psychological cravings will be minimal and intelligence will be the determining factor. Remember, in this approach to food selection we consider the taste influences and the governing principles of the body. This does not mean that foods to be avoided in special instances are not nutritious, but merely that they may tend to contribute to an increase of governing principles which you may not want to be predominant in your body. A general guideline is to provide all six tastes at each meal, with a predominance of tastes which have been chosen for special needs. During a family meal, or any group meal, it is usually possible to select from available foods those which suit your particular needs. When you are following a food regimen for special purposes, the variety of foods available for the menu is sufficient to ensure a balanced selection to meet nutritional needs, and in most instances vitamin and mineral supplementation will not be necessary.

Foods should be selected for freshness and be in their natural state. Processed foods should be avoided. Liquid foods, such as milk and juices, should be stored in opaque glass containers, not in clear glass containers or in plastic. Light can destroy vitamins in liquids and decrease their nutritional value.

Kitchen utensils and food containers should be made of natural materials, not plastic or aluminum. Everything used in the preparation of food should be clean, including the countertops, cutting boards, and cutting and mixing utensils. Vegetables and fruits should be washed, and unused grains and nuts kept in sealed containers.

Many foods can be eaten in their raw state and still be easily assimilated by the body; Some foods, however, are more useful to the body when cooked. When vegetables are cooked, heat causes the starch inside the cells to swell. This ruptures the cellulose walls of the plant cells and releases the nutrients. Cells are destroyed by heat, exposing their contents to oxidation.

SUGGESTED FOODS FOR WATER (Kapha) CONSTITUTIONAL TYPES

Avoiding breakfast until as least 10 A.M. Also, avoid sugar, fats, diary products, and salt, and to add lighter, drier foods. Lunch should be the major meal of the day, with only a light, dry meal in the evening. Also avoided cold drinks, large quantities of food, and indulgence in sweet, sour, and salty tastes. Occasional short fasts can be handled.

Vegetables	Fruits	Grains
pungent & bitter vegetables	apples	barley
asparagus	apricots	corn
beets	berries	millet
broccoli	cherries	oats, dry
brussels sprouts	cranberries	rye
cabbage	figs	basmati rice in small quantities
carrots	mangos	
cauliflower	peaches	
celery	pears	
eggplant	persimmon	All legumes
garlic	pomegranate	except kidney
leafy greens	prunes	beans, soybeans,
onions	raisins	and black lentils.
parsley		Clarified butter
peas		and goat's milk
peppers		all right.
potatoes		Almond, corn,
spinach		and sunflower oils in small quantities

The Water governing principle is aggravated in the spring of the year. At this time eat less and add more dry, fibrous foods.

SUGGESTED FOODS FOR FIRE (Pitta) CONSTITUTIONAL TYPES

Breakfast is usually all right for this constitutional type. Should avoid egg yolks, nuts, chilies, hot spices, honey, and hot drinks. Cool foods and liquids are better, and add sweet, bitter, and astringent tastes. Should avoid sour-tasting foods. Among spices, black pepper, coriander, and cardamom are all right.

Vegetables	Fruits	Grains
sweet & bitter vegetables O.K.	sweet fruits	barley
asparagus	apples	oats, cooked
broccoli	avocado	basmati rice
brussels sprouts	figs	wheta
cabbage	dark grapes	
cucumber	mangos	
cauliflower	melons	All legumes
celery	oranges	except lentils are
green beans	pineapple	all right.
leafy greens	plums	Coconut,
mushrooms	pomegranate	sunflower, and
okra	prunes	pumpkin seeds
peas	raisins	are all right.
parsley		Dairy products
green peppers		in moderation.
potatoes		Coconut, olive,
sprouts		soy, and sunflower
zucchini squash		oils.

The Fire governing principle is aggravated during summer. Stay calm and cool, increasing cooling foods and drinks.

SUGGESTED FOODS FOR AIR (Vata) CONSTITUTIONAL TYPES

Breakfast is usually all right and, sometimes, light meals during the day. Avoid dry and bitter foods. Sweet and hot foods are useful. Dairy products, in moderation, can usually be tolerated. These types should add more sweet and oily foods, as well as salty and sour tastes. Warm or hot water is all right. Nuts and nut butters are usually all right. Spices such as cinnamon, cardamom, cumin, ginger, cloves, and mustard can be used with benefit.

Vegetables	Fruits	Grains
cooked vegetables	sweet fruits	oats, cooked
asparagus	apricot	rice
beets	avocado	wheat
carrots	bananas	
cucumber	berries	
garlic cherries		
green beans	coconut	No legumes
onion, cooked	fresh figs	except mung
sweet potato	grapefruit	beans, black and
radishes	lemons	red lentils, and
leafy greens	grapes	tofu.
in moderation	mangos	All oils are all
	sweet melons	right.
	sour oranges	
	papaya	
	peaches	
	sour pineapple	
	sour plums	
	persimmons	

The Air governing principle is aggravated during autumn and winter. Increase warm and oily foods during this season.

For these reasons, cooked foods should be eaten soon after they are prepared and not stored for a long time afterwards.

Another advantage of cooking some foods is that when they are cooked they become more concentrated and the condensed cooked food contains more nutrients per unit volume than before being reduced by cooking. Usually, you must eat a relatively larger volume of raw foods because of their water content. The ideal, in most instances, is not to overcook or use extremely high heat when preparing vegetables.

An Easy Cleansing Routine to Use From Time to Time

At times you may feel the need to experience body cleansing. Fasting is not usually recommended for these purposes unless carefully supervised and suitable for the individual constitutional type. Air constitutional types should not fast very much, because they will experience an increase of the Air governing principle and become light-headed. Fire constitutional types can fast a few days, at most, because fasting often increases the Fire governing principle in the body, which will tend to aggravate it in a person who already has a strong Fire influence. Water constitutional types can usually fast more comfortably than other types.

An easy way to encourage the cleansing of toxic waste from the body is to simply consume only pure foods like fruits and vegetables. To start, plan ahead to help yourself to be psychologically prepared. This is not an extreme routine and will not interfere with your normal activities. During this regimen be sure to ensure intestinal cleansing. Also, bathe twice a day and obtain sufficient exercise. Extended daily walks are useful as exercise. Meditate on a regular schedule and feel that the inner life force is becoming increasingly influential in your body.

The morning meal can be fresh fruit or dried fruits which have been stewed or soaked overnight in water. Fruits are cleansers and supply nutrients in easily assimilated form.

The noon meal can be a fresh garden salad. For a dressing, lemon juice and olive oil can be used. If something more solid is desired, a small portion of cooked brown rice can be added to the meal. Chopped onion or garlic could be added to the rice.

The early evening meal could be another small fresh garden salad and a baked potato. To garnish the potato, use sauteed onion and garlic or any colorful vegetable topping.

After several days the body will feel light and clean, the eyes and tongue will be clean, and the stool will be odorless and will float in water. There will be an increase in energy and mental alertness, and meditation will be easy and enjoyable.

Everything in nature is built up of atomic particles—we live in an electric universe. Electric vital force is present in natural foods and is released into the body when foods are consumed. The beneficial ingredients of natural foods are transformed solar light. Electricity results in action, a breaking and making of equilibrium. Fruits attack and break up toxic conditions. Some vegetables such as potatoes and onions, on the other hand, attract toxic matter by magnetic force and carry it away from the body. This is why in this regimen, fruits are taken in the morning and vegetables later in the day.

After a suitable time you can begin to gradually include other preferred items in the diet, until the dietary program is once again established to suit personal preference and needs.

During the cleansing routine, and afterwards, distilled water is the preferred drink. It should always be stored in a glass, earthenware, or stainless steel container. Distilled water attracts waste matter, especially urea, and carries it out through the kidneys. Water is best taken at room temperature, rather than hot or cold, except for special purposes. Besides the influences of the governing principles of foods, also considered in this approach is whether foods and liquids are hot, cold, light, heavy, oily, or dry. Hot foods increase Fire influence. Cold fluids reduce Fire influence and increase Water influence. Light, dry foods increase Air influence and decrease Water influence. Heavy, oily foods increase the Water influence and decrease the Air influence. A person with a strong Fire constitution, for example, would be likely to aggravate his constitution by consuming too much hot and spicy food. Too much cold food and cold liquids would not be good for a Water type constitution, nor would too much heavy and oily food. Too much light, dry food would not be good for an Air constitution. We can understand, then, how indiscriminate choice of foods and liquids might be upsetting to body systems because of disturbing the balance of governing principles.

Warm cooked foods are suitable, while uncooked foods and liquids are best taken at near room temperature. Excess of any food or liquid is not recommended. Even herbal teas should not be used in excess, because they are "medicines," with their ingredients concentrated in water.

The Practical Benefits of Moderation in Diet

Eating foods in proper quantities and combinations ensures adequate nutrition, ideal body weight, an abundance of energy, and quite possibly a longer life span. Live foods, and life force taken in through breathing and meditation, provide nutrients and life force, and help maintain a balance of the governing principles in the body. Body weight stabilizes because underweight people gain and overweight people lose weight. By not overeating, the body conserves energy which would otherwise be used up in processing unnecessary foods.

There is evidence to indicate that planned undereating, that is, eating less than is the norm for most people, is helpful in many ways. The ideal of eating slowly, chewing well, and stopping before feeling full is a good way to monitor the appetite. Undereating does not mean malnutrition. It is simply a matter of eating what is required and no more. Naturally thin people often metabolize foods more quickly and have a higher body temperature, both of which may reduce life span. A person with slow metabolism who overeats may also have a reduced life span because of complications caused by overeating. The purpose of undereating is not to become thin, but to provide only what the body requires, and no excess. Unrestricted food intake may be linked to a variety of ailments, such as kidney and heart disease, cataracts, and cancer. The plan should be, then, to eat only when hungry and only what is necessary. Occasional cleansing routines can also be used to remove toxic wastes.

Some foods act as cleansers, some as builders, and some as vitalizers. Foods can be used and the effects carefully noted when these particular needs arise. Fruits are cleansers. Vegetables that grow above the ground are cleansing and sustaining foods. They have strong solar influence, but not as much as fruits which grow higher above the ground. Underground vegetables have more earth influence and are also sustaining foods. Potatoes, carrots, beets, turnips and other root vegetables fall into this category. Onions, garlic, and ginger are vitalizing foods, especially for men. They are also powerful cleansers and help in the removal of toxins and harmful bacteria from the body.

Nuts can be useful to the diet but should not be used to excess, since they are concentrated and high in fat content. A dozen almonds, for instance, is a sufficient quantity at one time, well chewed or blended with liquid. Some nuts are difficult to digest, so personal experimentation will be required. Peanuts (which are not really nuts, but legumes), for instance, are difficult to digest, as are soybeans. Undigested proteins, since they cannot be stored by the body, result in toxic residue which has to be flushed from the system.

The foods listed for each constitutional type are the ones which will not increase one's dominant governing principles while allowing the ones less influential to increase, thus contributing to harmony among them. When planning menus, experiment by partaking of the food groups recommended for your constitutional type to see if changes in the general feeling of well-being are noted.

For instance, if you have a mixed constitutional type, and your basic type is Water-Fire with Water predominant and only a small amount of Air influence present, you could select foods according to the percentages as determined from the self-examination test. For instance, if your basic constitutional type is fifty percent Water, thirty percent Fire, and twenty percent Air, foods could be selected from the Water, Fire, and Air listings accordingly. Vegetables, grains, and legumes should constitute the basic dietary plan. When grains, such as rice or corn, are eaten at the same time as beans or lentils, the combination enables the combined amino acids from these two groups to provide a balance of protein requirements. Fruits should be the smaller portion of the overall dietary routine and should not be eaten with the main meal for easier digestibility.

Fruit and vegetable juices should be used only in moderation, because they comprise the concentrated essence of a much larger volume of vegetables or fruits than you would ordinarily consume at one time. Fruit juices may be diluted by fifty percent with water to pose less of a challenge to the digestive process. Apple juice is good for Water constitutional types because it decreases Water and Fire and increases Air. Grape juice is good for Fire and Air types because it decreases these governing principles and increases Water influence. The guide is to choose juices in the same way you would select foods, using them according to the chart which best agrees with your basic type.

When using recipes, simply substitute foods which are more desirable for personal use when possible. An innovative food preparer will have no problem in planning attractive menus that will be pleasing in every way, while satisfying requirements for maintaining the balance of governing principles which influence body functions.

Remember, food is just one way of contributing to the balance of internal processes. Of utmost importance is attention to spiritual practices and the maintenance of a cheerful outlook and balanced mental attitude at all times.

Review

1. The principles of right living are shared in this chapter. They are easy to understand and require only personal discipline to be beneficial.
2. This system of wellness is researched, prevention-oriented, in most instances easily applied, free from harmful side-effects, economical, and aimed at treating the underlying causes of discomfort rather than merely suppressing symptoms.
3. Emphasis is upon the cultivation of spiritual awareness, the ordering of personal environment, behavior modification when necessary, and specific therapeutic strategies.
4. Review and understand the nature and influences of the governing principles in nature and in your body.
5. Food is consciousness. Select foods for nutritional value and for the "taste influences" upon your body's governing principles.
6. Strengthen your immune system and increase life essence through natural means and daily meditation.

SELF-EVALUATION AND PLANNING

1. Evaluate your basic constitutional nature by using the chart included in this chapter. Write the percentages.

   Water_____ Fire_____ Air_____

2. Based on what you have learned, write a program for yourself that includes spiritual practices, exercise routines, food routines, and whatever else will help you accomplish your purposes.

3. Write a daily routine for yourself. Include early morning routines, exercise routines, eating plans, and any other thing you can think of which might be useful for you to do.

4. If you do not have an avocation or extra interest which you enjoy, extend yourself and become interested in doing something which is interesting and life-enhancing.

When one knows thee, then alien there is
none, then no door is shut. Oh, grant me my
prayer that I may never lose the touch of the
one in the play of the many.
—*Rabindranath Tagore*

Delight thyself also in the Lord; and he shall
give thee the desires of thine heart. Commit
thy way unto the Lord; trust also in him;
and he shall bring it to pass.
—*Psalms 37:4,5*

There is a tide in the affairs of men, which, if
taken at the flood, leads on to fortune; omit-
ted, all the voyage of their lives is bound in
shallows and in miseries.
—*William Shakespeare*

Even on earth the world is transformed by
those whose minds are established in the vision of oneness.
—*Bhagavad Gita*

CHAPTER 7

What Shall We Do Now That We Know the Secrets of Forever Happiness?

Pause now, to think about how fortunate we are—how fortunate every person is who knows the way of inner happiness and fulfillment. This knowledge is beyond the price of anything available in the material worlds. It cannot be earned. It can only be known when intelligence is clear and a degree of inner awakening has been experienced.

Billions of people do not know some of the things you now know as a result of having read this book. And almost as many know nothing of the inner side of life. Because we ponder these matters, let us not feel any de-

gree of self-righteousness. Knowing about the truth of
life is one thing, but actually learning to let consciousness express in our lives is another, bringing with it the
need for increased personal responsibility. This is why
you have to ask yourself, "What shall I do now that I
know the secrets of forever happiness?"

Please ask this question of yourself right now. Contemplate it when you are quiet and alone. Listen deep
within to what your soul nature wants to reveal at the
conscious mind level. A superficial emotional response
will not be sufficient to enable you to see clearly what
your destiny with God is from this point in time. When
true guidance becomes apparent, it will bring with it
permanent realization and unshakable conviction.

Your way will be completely revealed to you,
sometimes immediately and sometimes over a period
of time during which inner guidance becomes more
clear and outer circumstances conform to such guidance. Follow your inner guidance with abiding faith.
The intelligence of God which brought you to your
present place in life will see you through the rest of the
way. Your willingness to rely more and more upon
grace, God's life expressive in our affairs, is evidence of
your increasing realization that you are indeed an-
chored in God—grounded in the vast field of limitless
consciousness which is the background and underlying
essence of the entire world process.

Are you sometimes insecure, even afraid? Don't
be, because the Power, which is also your life, knows
what is best for you even when you do not. It knows
your needs before you know them yourself. Provision
has already been made in the mind of God for your
near and distant future welfare. At a deep level, at the

level of your being, you know this to be so. Henceforth you can be wise, you can be practical, you can be patient when you need to be, and you can trust life. You will never be forsaken, overlooked, or deprived of grace.

Even when you are temporarily inept, even when you sometimes err, there is *something* which is ever with you, around you, and in you upon which you can rely.

The more you live out of an expanded state of consciousness and the more you open yourself to the opportunity of service to others, the more you will need to increase your awareness of God by deepening your spiritual practices. You will need the stability that only such practices can provide. There will be times when answers cannot be found in books or in the words of well-meaning friends. There will be times when only pure contemplation will satisfy your heart, your beingness. The real power of the ocean is in the depths, which cause surface appearances; and you must rest in the depths of the ocean of God-consciousness if you would experience all that you are destined to experience. Unfoldments will often occur in the most unplanned ways, so be watchful and alert to respond.

Prosper in All Ways and Live a Life of Service

Prosper—thrive, flourish, and be successful—in all areas of your life, and dedicate your life to the service of humanity and to assisting the purposes of evolution. Banish all restrictions from your consciousness, mind, body, and environment, and let the glory of God mani-

fest. You already know how to do these things; all that
is required now is that you do what you know to do.

Cultivate your prayer life. Clear your mind. Be
emotionally mature. Be physically healthy. Be supportive of your brothers and sisters on Planet Earth. Live a
life of conscious purpose. Meet needs. Heal hurts. Live
so that your life is an example to others. Give generously to life, just as life gives generously to you.

Remember that the Power of the universe, while at
times seeming to us to be personal, is also impersonal.
It will work through anyone who is open to It. The laws
of mental and spiritual creativity are not arbitrary, and
anyone who knows them can use them. Your good cannot be withheld from you when you are open to it. In
fact, you need not even pray for anything external to
yourself, because that which you desire for fuller expression is already available and needs only to be recognized and acknowledged. You do not need to visualize abundance, because there is no lack in the universe.
Learn to see *what is so* and relate to it. No amount of visualization or affirmation can improve upon the fact
that the world in which we live is already the energy of
consciousness manifesting.

Everything to which we relate in this world
emerged from the unmanifest field of consciousness,
and it will, sooner or later, dissolve into it. Therefore,
while we can use things, we cannot possess them. Even
the body we presently use will be taken away from us
in time. Time and space make possible the production
of the worlds and will also make possible its dissolu-
tion.

It is well to understand these matters, because
many of the problems common to human beings are

due to their vain attempts to hold on to things, to circumstances, to fleeting appearances making up the phenomenal realms.

So what will we do with our present and future opportunities? Will we continue as habit-bound persons, predictable because we are compelled by the force of drives and tendencies which govern us from unconscious levels of the mind, or will we welcome the invitation to awaken more fully to our spiritual potential and be consciously involved with unfolding events? The choice is before us. I hope you are making the correct one, the most useful one. If that choice is not made now, the force of evolution will bring you to the point of decision later on. Life will not allow you to remain unconscious and uncaring forever. We are impelled from within to extend ourselves in the direction of spiritual growth, and should we resist this impulse, circumstances about us will become so challenging that we will have to adjust attitudes and states of consciousness (and behavior) in order to adapt.

Experience fully your soul capacities, and intelligently use them to live the kind of life you are meant to live and to help others in the direction of their spiritual awareness and personal fulfillment.

Where your heart is, there will be your life. Your strongest feelings determine how you think, feel, relate, and behave. Examine your life. Isn't it true that everything you do is dictated by your present understanding and by what you feel is most important? The thoughts we think issue forth from our convictions, and our feelings support them. Our relationships reveal them. Our behavior in almost everything we do is an extension of what we feel deeply to be the most important to us.

Come to terms with this world. You are here for but a short time. You came from inner realms and you will return to them. Face up to this and let this understanding influence you.

Come to terms with people and nature. The same life flows through all of us, and through all of nature. The outer world is your larger body and you are just as responsible for it as you are the body you inhabit.

Come to terms with your duties. Perform them with skill and a cheerful heart. It is by performing our duties well that we render service to others, and to nature, and fulfill our earthly and spiritual obligations. Right where you are is your learning opportunity, and whether you "pass" or "fail" depends upon how well you perform.

Your every thought, your every feeling, your state of consciousness—all influence the fine and subtle fields of matter and consciousness around you, and throughout the universe. What kind of influence are you presently sharing? How are your actions influencing your world, in small or large measure?

Do practical things and be attentive to how you use time and resources. Being "very busy" is not always the best use of time if little or nothing results from being busy. At times, meditation and contemplation may be more useful, by making you more effective when you are engaged in activity.

Satisfying personal needs should not take too much time and effort. Do what you need to do to satisfy these needs and fulfill your responsibilities where you are, then extend yourself to serve the larger world community.

First, see to your own spiritual understanding and

all matters relating to wellness and function; you can only share with others what you, yourself, have.

Live a righteous life and radiate pure consciousness, always. According to your ability and resources, assist others in the direction of spiritual growth and total wellness. Society reflects the collective states of consciousness of all of its members, so do your part to be a good example to others and to contribute to the wellness of the whole. One of the advantages of being prosperous in all ways is that you no longer need to struggle to survive, or to forever overcome problems. You can, instead, cultivate the higher values and embody them.

Planetary consciousness is undergoing transformative growth-changes, and this process will continue for thousands of years; so let no one say he or she has nothing useful to do in this world. And while serving the cause of world enlightenment, remain inwardly centered so as not to become caught up in the very circumstances you are working to improve. Let compassion, not sentimental emotional involvement, be the guide. Let wisdom and right action prevail.

When you are, even to a mild degree, God-realized, you will be unselfish and void of all negative and destructive characteristics. You will be generous, loving, caring, and supportive of others and of worthy causes. As you selflessly serve your world, you will discover that your own spiritual growth is accelerated, even though this is not why you serve. You will experience the fulfillment which can only be known by yielding completely to the inclination of life to fulfill its purposes. Many struggle to find fulfillment in a variety of ways and never succeed, because fulfillment is not the result of doing "our will;" it occurs naturally when we do life's will.

When you come to the end of life's journey on Planet Earth, how well will you have played your role and how will you feel about what you have accomplished? Many do not even succeed in experiencing a satisfying human existence, because they do not know how to live, or they know how to live but allow inertia, distractions, and laziness to dominate their waking hours.

How about you? Are you living with clear purpose? Does your life have direction? Are you doing everything you should to contribute to the completion of purposes? Don't waste the opportunity you have now to experience life as it is meant to be. Never mind what others do, or do not do—you do what is right, and everything else will unfold in divine order.

A self-centered life is a destructive life—destructive for the person living it and harmful to all who are touched by it. On the other hand, a life lived with the understanding that infinite good is flowing to bless the world blesses the individual as well as the world. Be a blessing to the world by opening yourself to a continuous flow of good from the source.

Now that you know these principles, you are commissioned to exemplify them and share them with others. This is your spiritual duty, your responsibility, your rare privilege—and you are equal to it. Be thankful.